Getting Results with Accelerated Reader

The Accelerated products design, Accelerated Reader, AR, Accelerated Vocabulary, AR BookGuide, AR BookFinder, ATOS, Renaissance Home Connect, "Advanced Technology for Essential Practice," NEO 2, STAR Reading, STAR Early Literacy, and Renaissance Place are trademarks of Renaissance Learning, Inc., and its subsidiaries, registered, common law, or pending registration in the United States and other countries.

ISBN 978-1-59455-293-9
© 2007 by Renaissance Learning, Inc.
All rights reserved. Printed in the United States of America.

This publication is protected by U.S. and international copyright laws. It is unlawful to duplicate or reproduce any copyrighted material without authorization from the copyright holder. If this publication contains pages marked "Reproducible Form," only these pages may be photocopied and used by teachers within their own schools. They are not to be reproduced for private consulting or commercial use. For more information, contact:

Renaissance Learning, Inc.
2911 Peach Street
Wisconsin Rapids, WI 54494
(800) 338-4204
www.renlearn.com

Contents

Introduction 1

Accelerated Reader Basics

1. The Purpose of Accelerated Reader: Powerful Practice 5

Essential Practices

2. Assemble Resources 13
3. Personalize Reading Practice 16
4. Schedule Time for Reading and Quizzing 23
5. Manage Each Student's Reading Practice 26
6. Put Comprehension First 35
7. Make Success Visible 38
8. Spread the Joy of Reading 42

Managing AR in Your Classroom

9. Student Routines and Responsibilities 47
10. Teacher Routines 50
11. Common Questions 52

When You're Ready to Do More

12. Set Additional Goals 57
13. Enhance Practice and Analyze Data More Deeply 60

Appendix

Instructions for Common Software Tasks 67
Reproducible Forms 76

Index 90

Introduction

Congratulations! You have purchased one of the most effective software tools for fostering reading growth—Accelerated Reader. As with all tools, the results that you and your students achieve with AR will depend on what you do with it. When used casually, AR helps students' reading abilities grow. When used thoughtfully and with proven techniques, it leads to tremendous gains and a lifelong love of reading.

In this book, we describe some of the techniques that maximize the potential of Accelerated Reader. First, we give you basic information about the purpose of AR and its essential concepts. Then we describe the practices that will get you and your students off to a good start. After that, we provide tips for managing your classroom, and finally, we describe other practices that we encourage you to do when you're ready. The appendix contains step-by-step instructions for the most common software tasks.

We hope what you find here will inform and inspire you. Bear in mind, however, that this is only an introduction. To learn more about other professional-development opportunities, visit our website: www.renlearn.com.

Accelerated Reader Basics

1

The Purpose of Accelerated Reader: Powerful Practice

Reading is a skill and, as with every skill, it requires not just instruction but practice. Reading practice serves a number of purposes. It enables students to apply the skills and strategies that you teach. It gives you opportunities to check student learning and identify weaknesses. And it draws students into the world of "real" reading—a world in which people learn from and enjoy books.

Practice does not automatically lead to growth, however. To be effective, practice must have certain attributes: It must be at the right level of difficulty, cover a sufficient amount of time, be guided by the instructor, and be enjoyable enough to sustain.

The purpose of Accelerated Reader is to enable powerful practice. It does this by:

- Providing data that helps you monitor and personalize reading practice.
- Encouraging substantial amounts of practice, according to guidelines based on research findings.
- Making practice fun for students by facilitating successful encounters with text.

Accelerated Reader and Your Curriculum

Accelerated Reader is designed to be part of a comprehensive reading program. It does not replace basal-reader series or other instructional materials; rather, it supports and enhances them. As the National Reading Panel stated in its 2000 report, *Teaching Children to Read*, effective reading programs are balanced: Students receive direct and systematic instruction in phonemic awareness, phonics skills, and comprehension strategies, and they are given opportunities to apply their knowledge in a variety of "natural settings." One of the primary benefits of Accelerated Reader is that it is a vehicle for this essential learning transfer.

Accelerated Reader provides other research-proven benefits as well. It promotes wide reading, which is the most effective method for building vocabulary. And through its progress-monitoring and feedback mechanisms, it reinforces student effort—one of the most important practices in classrooms that work, according to education expert Robert Marzano. Supported by a vast body of scientific research, AR has been favorably reviewed by the What Works Clearinghouse and the National Center on Student Progress Monitoring.

How Accelerated Reader Works

At the heart of Accelerated Reader are a few basic steps:

1. You schedule time for daily reading practice, additional to your instructional reading period. During this time, your students select and read library books that match their individual ability levels and interests.
2. When a student finishes a book, he or she takes an AR Reading Practice Quiz on the computer. This quiz assesses general comprehension of the book just read.
3. Accelerated Reader scores the quiz, keeps track of the results, and generates reports. You use this data to monitor each student's practice, guide students to appropriate books, and target instruction.

What Guided Independent Reading Looks Like

Guided independent reading is an active classroom practice for students *and* for you, with a number of activities taking place at the same time. Typically, most students will be reading quietly to themselves. A few students will be taking AR quizzes at computer stations in a corner of the classroom. Other students will be selecting a new book to read, either from the classroom library or the school library.

Meanwhile, you will be circulating around the room, monitoring, coaching, and intervening. Students who have finished a book will come to you and ask permission to take a quiz. Students who have just taken a quiz will show you the results so that you can confer with the student, reinforce good work, and provide guidance on

which book to choose next. While students read, you will move from individual to individual, checking to see that their books are a good fit, reinforcing concepts and skills you may have taught during a lesson, and showing your interest in them and their efforts.

Because you will have established routines for all these things, which we'll describe later in this book, students can work independently and in an orderly fashion.

Key Concepts

For practice to be personalized, there must be a good match between the individual and whatever the individual needs to practice with. That means there must be a way to measure both these elements. Think of working with a personal trainer at the gym: He has to assess your physical capabilities, and he needs to understand his exercise equipment so he can recommend a workout that's just right for you. With AR, we measure students' reading capabilities, and we measure the "equipment" they use—books. In this section, we describe those measurements. In a later section, we'll give you more details on how to use them on a day-to-day basis.

Zone of Proximal Development

Common sense tells us that whenever we practice a skill, we will get the most from our efforts if we work at the right level. If, for example, a 50-year-old woman is new to weight training, 10-pound weights will likely be more suitable than 30-pound weights. On the other hand, if an athletic 20-year-old practiced only with 10-pound weights, she likely wouldn't develop to her full potential.

The same principle applies to reading. Practicing with books that are too hard results in frustration. Practicing with books that are too easy does little to improve skills and leads to boredom. With AR, we use the term zone of proximal development, or ZPD, to match students to appropriate books. Based on a concept developed by Russian psychologist Lev Vygotsky, the ZPD represents the level of difficulty that is neither too hard nor too easy, and is the level at which optimal learning takes place.

When you begin using AR, you will need baseline data on each student's reading ability in order to estimate a ZPD. Any standardized reading assessment, including STAR Reading, provides this baseline data. STAR Reading also suggests a ZPD for each student. This suggestion is a personalized starting place for reading practice and may need to be adjusted over time. It's just like working with the personal trainer. He'll do an initial assessment to get you going. But he'll monitor you closely and make adjustments to your practice routine so that you continuously work within the zone of difficulty that will lead to the greatest gains.

> **Alternate Book-Level Scales**
>
> AR works with multiple reading measures. If you have AR 7.5 or higher, you can set a preference in the software so that it displays book levels on a 2,000- or 100-point scale rather than the ATOS grade-level scale. If you set this preference, the scale you choose will be used wherever a book level is shown. This includes book labels; software screens, such as the Class Record Book; and reports that show student data. See the software manual for instructions.

Book Level, Interest Level, and Points

To help you guide students to books that are right for them, we provide three pieces of information about every book for which we have an AR quiz:

- **Book Level** represents the difficulty of the text. It is determined by a readability formula called ATOS, which analyzes the average length of the sentences in the book, the average length of the words, and the average grade level of the words. ATOS reports the overall book level in terms of grade. For example, a book level of 4.5 means that the text could likely be read by a student whose reading skills are at the level of grade four, fifth month of the school year. It does not, however, mean that the content is appropriate for a fourth-grader. To indicate that, we use another measure called "interest level."

- **Interest Level** is based on content—a book's themes and ideas—and indicates for which age group a book is appropriate. In many cases, a book's interest level coordinates with its book level. *Hank the Cowdog*, for example, which is suitable for fourth-graders, has a book level of 4.5. Many books, however, have a low book level but are appropriate for higher grades and vice versa. For example, Ernest Hemingway's *The Sun Also Rises* has a book level of 4.4 because the sentences are short and the vocabulary is simple. The interest level, however, is UG or Upper Grades. *Arthur Throws a Tantrum,* on the other hand, with an interest level of LG or Lower Grades, has a book level of 4.9 because it contains fairly long words and sentences.

The chart below shows which grades fall into each interest level.

Interest Level	Grade Appropriateness
LG	Lower Grades, K–3
MG	Middle Grades, 4–8
UG	Upper Grades, 9–12

- **Points** are assigned to each book based on its length and difficulty. For example, the Berenstain Bears books, which are about 8,000 words long, are 1-point books. *Hank the Cowdog*, which is about 23,000 words long, is a 3-point book. *The Sun Also Rises*, about 70,000 words long, is a 10-point book. The formula for calculating points is:

AR points = [(10 + book level)/10] x (words in book/10,000)

As you work with AR, you will notice that some popular books have more points assigned to them than some classic pieces of literature. Tom Clancy's *Executive Orders*, for example, is a 78-point book while Shakespeare's *Macbeth* is a 4-point book. Keep in mind that this doesn't mean we think *Executive Orders* is a better book or more worthwhile to read than *Macbeth*. Points only tell you that *Executive Orders*—at more than a thousand pages— is much longer than Shakespeare's masterpiece play.

[Handwritten note: Key — 85% or higher in quiz average to keep up at their grade level.]

AR Measures Practice with Points

Because points are based on word count, AR uses them to keep track of how much reading a student has done. Students "earn" points by taking the AR quiz for the book they have just read. If a student reads a 10-point book and scores 100 percent on the quiz, he earns 100 percent of the points. If the student scores 90 percent, he earns 90 percent of the points, and so on. To earn any amount of points, a student must score at least 60 percent on a 5- or 10-question quiz and 70 percent on a 20-question quiz. Points make it easy to see how much reading practice a student has successfully completed. For example, a student who has accumulated 50 points has read many more words than a student who has accumulated 10 points.

Potential Problems with Points

In sports and other competitions, a player wins by earning more points than anybody else. Sometimes schools approach AR in the same way and recognize students who earn the most points. We discourage this practice. It's true that a student who has earned a large number of points has done quite a bit of reading, and that's good. But when schools focus primarily on points a couple of things tend to happen:

- Students choose inappropriate books. In their zeal to earn points and rewards, able readers read dozens of easy low-point books; struggling readers choose high-point books that are too difficult. All students lose sight of the primary goal, which is to read interesting books at the level of difficulty that is right for each of them as individuals.
- When all students pursue the same goal—to earn the most points—less skilled readers are handicapped. Since only a few students "win," those who feel they can never win give up.
- Students cheat. To try to earn more points, they take quizzes without reading books, and they share answers.

Instead of encouraging students to compete for points, we recommend that you set personalized point goals. These take into account each student's ability level and enable every student to succeed and grow. We'll explain how to do this later.

The Importance of Good Comprehension

Our research shows that the most important factor in accelerated reading growth is good comprehension. Therefore we encourage students to strive for high scores on AR quizzes and maintain an average score of at least 85 percent—with 90 percent being even better.

Why then, you may be wondering, does AR give students points for scores of 60 percent and higher, if an average of 85 or 90 percent is the goal? Remember, points tell you how much reading practice a student has done. If a student spends two weeks reading a 10-point book and scores 100 percent, AR records 10 points, which is a fantastic accomplishment. If the student only scores 60 percent, AR records 6 points, which is not so good but does document the time and effort he put in. The teacher's role, which we'll describe in a later chapter, is to either guide the student to a more appropriate book and/or help the student develop comprehension strategies so that he will be more successful with future books and quizzes.

Summary

AR KEY CONCEPTS

- The purpose of Accelerated Reader is to enable powerful practice.
- A student's ZPD represents the level of difficulty that is neither too hard nor too easy.
- Book level indicates the difficulty of text, not the maturity of content.
- Interest level tells you for which grade levels a book's themes and ideas are appropriate.
- Points are assigned to a book based primarily on its length. The number of points a student earns tells you how much reading a student has done.
- The most important factor in accelerated reading growth is good comprehension.

Essential Practices

Assemble Resources

Before you begin using Accelerated Reader, make sure the software is set up and you're familiar with it. Also check to see if you are using the desktop or web version since the instructions for using the programs are different. (The web version is powered by a program called Renaissance Place, which manages all of a school or district's Renaissance Learning software. If the Welcome screen says Renaissance Place when you log in, you have the web-based version.) Then survey your supply of books and computers. Prepare your books for student use and figure out how you can give students ready access to computers.

Prepare to Use the Software

Your technology staff needs to set up student, class, teacher, and school-year information in the software before you begin using it. If you have the Renaissance Place version of AR, they will also give you a user name and password, along with the web address (or URL) for the Renaissance Place home page. Once you have this information, log in by following the instructions in the appendix. Notice that there are separate instructions for the Renaissance Place and desktop versions of the software as well as for using NEO 2 laptops.

Identify Student User Names and Passwords

If you have the Renaissance Place version of AR, each of your students is assigned a user name and password, which can be found on the Student Information Report. If you are using the desktop version of the software, each student has a password; these are found on the Student List Report. Print these reports and give the information to your students. See the appendix for instructions.

Take a Sample Quiz

AR includes different types of quizzes for different purposes. The quiz of basic comprehension that students take on books they select for reading practice is called a Reading Practice Quiz. Familiarize yourself with this type of quiz by taking one on a book that you know. (See the appendix for instructions on logging in as a student, taking a quiz, and aborting a quiz.) A Reading Practice Quiz consists of 5, 10, or 20 multiple-choice questions, depending on the length and complexity of the book.

> **Other Quiz Formats and Types**
>
> Reading Practice Quizzes are available with audio for many primary-level books, and in Spanish for best-selling Spanish titles. Other types of quizzes are available as well: Vocabulary Practice Quizzes test student knowledge of key vocabulary words in books students choose for independent reading, Literacy Skills Quizzes assess student proficiency with higher-level reading skills, and Other Reading Quizzes check comprehension of reading you assign in specific textbook series. See our website for details.

Label Books

In order for students to select books that are right for them, all the books for which you have AR quizzes must be labeled with their book level, interest level, and point value. It's also very helpful to have the AR quiz number on the label so that students can identify the right quiz when they are ready to take it.

You can print labels from the software or you can purchase preprinted labels through our website. As an alternative to labeling, some schools have a rubber stamp made with the words "Book Level," "Interest Level," "Points," and "Quiz Number." They stamp the inside cover of each book and write in the information. To streamline book selection for younger students, you may want to color-code primary-grade books by using colored dots in half- or whole-grade increments. (A color-coding system is not recommended for books for older students since struggling readers may not want the level of the books they are reading to be visible to others. Label books for older students with plain labels instead.)

Make Sure You Have Enough Books and Quizzes

Once you begin implementing Accelerated Reader, you and your librarian can expect library circulation to rise dramatically. The chart on this page gives guidelines that will help you make sure your school has enough books to keep students fully occupied with reading practice. A deep and broad collection also ensures that students will find appealing books that will motivate them to read more.

Keep in mind that GE refers to a student's grade-equivalent reading level, not grade in school. That means, for example, that if your school has a high proportion of students reading at lower levels, the librarian will want to adjust her book acquisition program accordingly. Note that the number of books needed is higher for lower GEs; that's because beginning readers read short books that they finish quickly. If you test your students with STAR Reading, print the Summary Report to see how many students are reading at various GE levels.

Also make sure you have a Reading Practice Quiz for as many books as possible. If your school has the Enterprise Edition of Accelerated Reader, you have access to every quiz available. Otherwise, you can order quizzes through vendors or our online store. In addition, your librarian may wish to order BookGuide. This program can be linked to your school library's circulation system to identify books in your collection that are missing quizzes, and quizzes you already own for which you need matching books.

Recommended Number of Books	
GE	AR Books per Student
0.0 – 1.9	10
2.0 – 2.9	8
3.0 – 5.9	5
6.0 – 8.9	4
9.0+	2

Figure Out Computer Access for Student Quizzing

We recommend that students take a quiz within 24 hours of finishing a book. If students have to wait longer to quiz and they do poorly, you won't know if they had problems comprehending what they read or if they simply forgot some of the details. Therefore, having one or more computers in each classroom is optimum. Some schools set up additional computers in the library. If you have AR 7.5 or higher and NEO 2 laptops, students can take quizzes right at their desks. After quizzing, students send their responses to AR software via a wireless receiver. The results are incorporated into the database and appear on reports as they normally would. You will also need a printer to print quiz results.

Arrange for Library Access

Students need easy access to the library so that as soon as they finish a book, they can select another. A pass system works well. It allows students to go to the library individually, not just as a class, while controlling the number of students who are out of the classroom at one time. (The Student Reading Log, which we describe in a later chapter, is often used as a pass.) Because circulation increases dramatically with AR, your librarian will likely need additional helpers, such as student and parent volunteers, to assist with book selection and checkout. We strongly suggest that you also have a collection of books in your room. These books must also be labeled. In some schools, the librarian augments classroom libraries by sending out rotating book collections in crates or on carts.

Prepare Your Room

Devote a corner of the classroom to books and reading. Create an inviting nook with squares of carpeting, beanbag chairs, and perhaps an old sofa. Organize books by level on shelves or in crates, and add a display of great reads, as recommended by peers. Depending on the age group you're teaching, you might include a catchy sign: "Starbooks Café" was one teacher's choice.

> **Summary**
>
> **ASSEMBLE RESOURCES**
> - Identify student user names and passwords.
> - Take a sample quiz.
> - Label books.
> - Make sure you have enough books and quizzes.
> - Figure out computer access for student quizzing.
> - Arrange for library access.
> - Prepare your room.

Personalize Reading Practice

The most exciting feature of AR is that it makes it easy for you to personalize your student's reading practice. No more guesswork, no more Sunday-night planning sessions trying to match the right materials to the right student. If you want to see your students' reading skills soar, don't delay this important aspect of AR. Below we describe the steps: (1) Get baseline data on each student's reading ability. (2) Start each student at the level that seems about right, according to that baseline data, and fine-tune as needed. (3) Look up our recommendations for how much reading each student should do, depending on individual ability.

Use a STAR Assessment for Baseline Data

STAR Reading and STAR Early Literacy are reading assessments that give baseline data on each student's reading ability. When used periodically throughout the school year, they also measure growth. To take a STAR Reading assessment, students need a sight vocabulary of at least 100 words; STAR Early Literacy is designed for students who are not yet reading independently.

Administer STAR assessments to students as early as possible in the school year. Both tests are computerized and deliver results immediately. We recommend using a computer lab so that you can provide a quiet environment and your entire class can be tested at one time. Be sure to print the pretest instructions, which you can read to students to explain how the test works. You'll find the pretest instructions by clicking the Manuals link in the upper-right corner of the program.

Identify Each Student's Initial ZPD

In addition to providing information on a student's overall reading ability, STAR Reading also suggests a range of book levels for each student—a ZPD. The ZPD that is provided by STAR Reading is a personalized *starting place* for reading practice.

You'll find suggested ZPDs listed for all your students on STAR's Reading Range Report. (See the appendix for instructions on viewing STAR Reports.) If you do not have STAR Reading, use the grade-equivalent (GE) score from any reading assessment and the chart on the following page to identify each student's initial ZPD. If no test is available, estimate grade-equivalency by observing what the student is able to read. (A chart that shows ZPDs on a 2,000-point scale is in the appendix.)

Grade-Equivalent Reading Score	Suggested ZPD
1.0	1.0 – 2.0
1.5	1.5 – 2.5
2.0	2.0 – 3.0
2.5	2.3 – 3.3
3.0	2.6 – 3.6
3.5	2.8 – 4.0
4.0	3.0 – 4.5
4.5	3.2 – 5.0
5.0	3.4 – 5.4
5.5	3.7 – 5.7
6.0	4.0 – 6.1
6.5	4.2 – 6.5
7.0	4.3 – 7.0
7.5	4.4 – 7.5
8.0	4.5 – 8.0
9.0	4.6 – 9.0
10.0	4.7 – 10.0
11.0	4.8 – 11.0
12.0	4.9 – 12.0

Why ZPD Covers a Range of Levels

We express the ZPD as a range. Rather than tell you, for example, that a student should practice reading books at a 2.8 level, we might suggest a ZPD of 2.8 to 4.0. There are two reasons for this.

1. Identifying a student's ZPD is not an exact science. People are too complex, and the reading process too dynamic, for us to tell you precisely which level book would be most suitable for a particular child. Experiential background, vocabulary, culture, and interests all affect how hard or easy a book is to read.
2. It's important that students have a large variety of books from which to choose. This allows them to pursue their interests and results in the most authentic and motivating reading experience.

We urge you not to strictly control students' choices within their ZPDs. While you might be tempted to have a student first read books at a 2.8 level, then a 2.9 level, 3.0 level, and so on, research does not show that this kind of progression with library books leads to greater gains. The practice also severely limits a student's choices and turns reading into a chore.

How ZPDs Are Configured

When you look at the chart and compare grade-equivalent scores to ZPDs, you'll see a distinctive pattern. Above 2.0, the ZPD begins at a level that is lower than the GE—considerably lower as the GE goes up. For example, if a student has a GE of 8.0, the suggested ZPD is 4.5 to 8.0. This is because the GE from a test represents the highest level at which a student can read short passages, not the level at which he or she can read comfortably for hours. Besides that, most recreational reading material is written at a level below 6.0. If students were asked to only read books that matched their GE, once they tested higher than about 6.0, they would be faced with very difficult—and probably not very enjoyable—material.

Consider the situation in adult terms. While a college graduate might have a GE of 12.0+, books written at that level are likely to be textbooks. In contrast, Stephen King's *The Shining* has a book level of 5.8 and John Steinbeck's *The Grapes of Wrath* has a book level of 4.9.

Use the Concept of ZPD to Guide Reading Practice

The ZPD is central to guiding reading practice. Once you identify initial ZPDs with a STAR Reading assessment or through other means, you'll want your students to start out reading at those levels. You will also monitor their reading closely to see whether these initial ZPDs are good fits or whether you need to make adjustments. This is how reading practice is personalized—through your careful observation.

Make Sure Students Know Their ZPD
A fundamental principle of Accelerated Reader—and effective education, in general—is that students must become self-directed learners. For this reason, they must know their own ZPD so they can select books that fall within their range. (Most AR forms have a spot to record ZPD.) You will find that this kind of involvement builds a sense of self-control in students and is highly motivating. You will also discover that students acquire an understanding of what is the right level of challenge for them. As a result, students themselves can provide valuable input as you guide their reading practice.

Quiz Averages of at Least 85 Percent Show Students Are Reading in Their Zone
The ZPD that STAR Reading reports may—or may not—be the right ZPD for an individual student. No single testing event can be guaranteed to be perfectly accurate. It's just like seeing that personal trainer: If you are tired or distracted the day you go in for an initial assessment, his conclusions about your fitness level may not be exactly right. That's why the most important indicator of your capabilities is what you actually can accomplish in each training session. It's also why the best indicator of a student's reading ability is how well the student does with daily reading practice.

Once you have identified a student's ZPD and the student reads and takes quizzes on books within that range, you will begin receiving data from AR about the student's comprehension. The quizzes act like a heart monitor—they give you information that tells you how hard the student is working.

We know from our research that if a student is able to maintain an average score on AR Reading Practice Quizzes of at least 85 percent, the student is working at the optimum level of difficulty. That means if a student is unable to achieve an average of 85 percent, you would first look at the student's technique: Is she applying basic comprehension strategies? If the technique is good but the student continues to struggle, you would then guide the student to lower-level books. As the student's skills improve, open up the higher end of the range from which the student is choosing books to encourage more challenging reading.

For example, let's say Sally's STAR Reading test score suggests a ZPD of 3.0 to 4.5. Sally reads two books—one at a 3.0 level and one at a 3.3 level—but she does poorly on the quizzes, averaging only 65 percent. Her teacher, Mrs. Brown, coaches Sally to summarize in her head what she's read each day, and to briefly review a book before she quizzes. However, Sally continues to score low. Mrs. Brown concludes that Sally's ZPD is a bit lower than the one suggested by STAR Reading and asks her to choose books with a book level of 2.2 to 2.8. Sally reads a number of books within this new range, averages 90 percent, and gains confidence. Mrs. Brown has another conversation with Sally, who says she's ready to once again try harder books. Mrs. Brown guides her to books written at a level of 2.2 to 3.2. By opening up the top end of the range while keeping the low end the same, Mrs. Brown encourages more challenging reading but still allows Sally to read books with which she knows she will be successful.

When you first start using AR, you may wish that there were more definite "rules" for establishing ZPDs and guiding book-level choices. The truth is, students are too individual for rules to work. When to recommend lower- or higher-level books, how far to widen a book-level range—these decisions depend on many factors. The only hard-and-fast guidelines we can give you are:

- Get to know your students.
- Aim to keep them involved in reading practice that is successful and enjoyable, that builds confidence, and that advances their skills.
- Remember AR quizzes are like a heart monitor: Keep an eye on the data, and if a student can maintain an average of at least 85 percent, he or she is working at the right level.

ZPD and Emergent Readers
Students who are not yet reading independently will be practicing reading with books that are read to or with them. These emergent readers can also take AR quizzes, with the help of someone who reads the questions to or with them. You can use the AR data the same way you would with independent readers. Keep an eye on the level of book each student is choosing and the student's performance. If a student can maintain an average of at least 85 percent on AR quizzes, the books the student is listening to or reading with someone are at the right level of difficulty—that is, within the student's ZPD.

At the primary level, ZPD can be too abstract a term for students to use, however. Even a numerical grade level (1.2, for example) is hard for children of this age to grasp. If you color-code primary-level books, as we suggest in an earlier chapter, you can refer to book levels by color. Then it becomes easy for a student to understand that "yellow-dot books" are just right for him to listen to and, when he's ready, he can move into "blue-dot books."

Personalize Practice with Individual Point Goals

If a trainer were to create a fitness program for you, he would specify not only how hard you should exercise but also how much exercise you should do. Reading practice needs to be regulated in the same way. AR makes this easy. As we just described, you regulate the difficulty of a student's reading practice through the ZPD. You regulate quantity with points.

What's the appropriate quantity? To find that out, we conducted extensive research to determine the amount of reading practice students must engage in to achieve growth. We measured the amount in time and found that 20 to 60 minutes a day of high-quality practice was associated with the greatest gains. We also kept track of how many points students of varying abilities accumulated within those 20 to 60 minutes. That's how we can estimate the number of points students need to earn in order to advance their skills.

We summarize these findings in our Goal-Setting Chart, which is shown below. (A reproducible chart is in the appendix.) You'll see that we expect skilled readers to accumulate more points within 30 minutes than less able readers. That makes sense. If you're a track star, you can cover a lot more ground in half an hour than a couch potato. And if you were coaching these two individuals, you would ask the track star to log more miles than the novice runner.

chart includes class time use

Grade-Equivalent Score	Suggested ZPD	60 Min. Daily Practice			30 Min. Daily Practice			20 Min. Daily Practice		
		Points per Week	Points per 6 Weeks	Points per 9 Weeks	Points per Week	Points per 6 Weeks	Points per 9 Weeks	Points per Week	Points per 6 Weeks	Points per 9 Weeks
1.0	1.0 – 2.0	1.7	10	15	0.9	5.0	7.5	0.6	3.3	5.0
1.5	1.5 – 2.5	1.9	11	17	1.0	5.5	8.5	0.6	3.7	5.7
2.0	2.0 – 3.0	2.1	13	19	1.1	6.5	9.5	0.7	4.3	6.3
2.5	2.3 – 3.3	2.3	14	21	1.2	7.0	10.5	0.8	4.7	7.0
3.0	2.6 – 3.6	2.5	15	23	1.3	7.5	11.5	0.8	5.0	7.7
3.5	2.8 – 4.0	2.7	16	24	1.4	8.0	12.0	0.9	5.3	8.0
4.0	3.0 – 4.5	2.8	17	25	1.4	8.5	12.5	0.9	5.7	8.3
4.5	3.2 – 5.0	3.2	19	29	1.6	9.5	14.5	1.0	6.3	9.7
5.0	3.4 – 5.4	3.5	21	32	1.8	10.5	16.0	1.2	7.0	10.7
5.5	3.7 – 5.7	3.9	23	35	2.0	11.5	17.5	1.3	7.7	11.7
6.0	4.0 – 6.1	4.2	25	39	2.1	12.5	19.5	1.4	8.3	13.0
6.5	4.2 – 6.5	4.6	28	41	2.3	14.0	20.5	1.5	9.3	13.7
7.0	4.3 – 7.0	4.9	29	44	2.5	14.5	22.0	1.6	9.7	14.7
7.5	4.4 – 7.5	5.3	32	48	2.7	16.0	24.0	1.8	10.7	16.0
8.0	4.5 – 8.0	5.6	34	50	2.8	17.0	25.0	1.9	11.3	16.7
9.0	4.6 – 9.0	6.3	38	57	3.2	19.0	28.5	2.1	12.7	19.0
10.0	4.7 – 10.0	6.9	41	62	3.5	20.5	31.0	2.3	13.7	20.7
11.0	4.8 – 11.0	7.6	46	68	3.8	23.0	34.0	2.5	15.3	22.7
12.0	4.9 – 12.0	8.3	50	75	4.2	25.0	37.5	2.8	16.7	25.0

How to Set Individual Point Goals
The procedure for setting individual point goals is simple. First, find a student's GE or ZPD on the Goal-Setting Chart. Then look across the chart to the column that matches the amount of time you are providing for practice. You'll see recommended point goals for a week or a marking period. With younger students, you might want to set goals by the week. For older students, who are reading longer books and are more able to work toward long-term goals, marking-period goals may be more suitable. You can enter individual point goals in the software, and AR will keep track of each student's progress. (The appendix gives instructions.) These goals must be for a marking period. If you are just starting out, however, and this sounds too complicated, you can still give students point goals that they note on paper. In the next section, we'll show you an example of a reading log that has space for a point goal.

You might find that some students and parents question the idea of setting different point goals for different students. If they do, you might use the analogy with them of the track star and the novice runner. To expect the novice to cover the same amount of ground as the track star would be setting him up for failure. Asking the track star to only run as much as the novice would be unfair to the track star: She likely would never reach her full potential.

Point Goals for Emergent and Beginning Readers
The Goal-Setting Chart is intended for independent readers. For students not yet reading on their own or just beginning to read, we recommend more generalized goals: At least .5 points per week for students in kindergarten, and .75 points for first-graders per 30 minutes of daily practice with books read to or with them.

Point Goals for High-Ability Readers
Some of your students may have a grade-equivalent score that is considerably higher than their grade in school. For example, you may have a sixth-grader with a GE of 12.0. If you followed the guidelines on the Goal-Setting Chart exactly, that student's point goal would be 37.5 points for 30 minutes of daily reading during a nine-week marking period. This goal is probably too high. We have found that the content of the long, complicated, high-point books that would enable a student to earn this many points is often too mature for younger students, even though they are capable of decoding the words. In addition, for students reading far above grade level, quantity of reading practice isn't as important as maintaining and broadening interest in reading. For these reasons, when you work with high-ability readers, we recommend that you set point goals that are more in line with their grade in school or perhaps a little higher. For example, think of a sixth-grader with a GE of 12.0 as reading solidly "on grade level" or 6.0. Looking at the Goal-Setting Chart, you'll see that the recommended point goal for a GE of 6.0 for 30 minutes of daily reading during a nine-week marking period is 19.5. This represents a goal the student can easily achieve without feeling pressured.

Adjusting Point Goals

Just like book-level ranges, point goals are not set in stone. Sometimes students work hard and yet struggle to meet a point goal. They may be absent a lot, or they may be English language learners who read more slowly than average. It's okay to lower a point goal. Use your best judgment, and set a goal that is realistic, motivating, and achievable.

Accelerated Reader and Grades

We do not recommend giving grades for reading practice; however, we do know many schools, especially high schools, choose to do so. If you must give grades for AR work, we encourage you to follow these guidelines:

- *Do* base a student's grade on the amount of progress made toward personalized goals. *Don't* give the highest grades to the highest point earners, which would unfairly penalize struggling readers.
- *Don't* grade students unless you are actively monitoring their work. Students who are scoring low on quizzes or accumulating few points usually need your guidance. They may be having trouble finding appropriate books, or they may be trying to read books that are too hard. Intervene first, and be sure students know what to do to be successful before evaluating their efforts.
- *Do* build your library and quiz collection before instituting a grading policy. Don't inadvertently turn students off to reading by forcing them to read books they aren't interested in simply to earn a good grade.
- *Do* make your library accessible so that students have ample opportunity to find books quickly and easily.
- If a number of teachers are using AR, *do* decide on a grading formula together.

For more information about Accelerated Reader and grades, attend one of our professional-development seminars.

Summary

PERSONALIZE READING PRACTICE
- Administer STAR Reading assessments and identify initial ZPDs.
- Explain ZPD to students.
- Set individual point goals.
- Understand that quiz-score averages of at least 85 percent show students are reading in their ZPD.
- As needed, adjust the level of the books students are reading so that they can achieve and maintain a high quiz average.

Schedule Time for Reading and Quizzing

Our research shows that students gain the most when they practice reading every day. For independent readers, we recommend scheduling at least 30 minutes in elementary and middle school and at least 20 minutes in high school. Emergent readers also require at least 30 minutes of daily practice, although this will likely be a combination of listening to someone read to them and assisted reading. Bear in mind that "practice" means reading AR books that students select themselves and is in addition to the reading students do in basal readers or other instructional materials.

Make In-School Reading Practice a Priority

Finding 20 to 30 minutes a day to devote exclusively to reading practice can be a challenge. But as with all goals, the stronger your commitment, the more likely you are to achieve success. Here are some things to try.

- **Enlist the support of your principal.** Ask your principal to schedule a time for the entire school to practice reading. Doing so creates a culture in which reading is valued and ensures that practice will take place.
- **Increase classroom efficiency.** Take a look at daily housekeeping chores, such as taking attendance and collecting homework. Can you make these more efficient?
- **Look at the daily schedule.** Does it include homeroom, study hall, or other time you can allocate to reading?
- **In middle or high school,** build reading into English classes, consider shortening each period, or reduce pass time between classes. In some schools, content-area teachers take turns providing time for reading practice.

Reading To, Reading With, and Reading Independently

Emergent readers spend most of their reading time listening to stories. As their skills develop, they may be paired with peers or adult tutors who read with them. Finally, as students' skills develop, they transition to independent reading. When a student reaches this stage, however, "reading to" and "reading with" activities need not be dropped. In fact, reading to students of all ages is a highly motivating way to introduce students to interesting books, model good reading behaviors, and promote discussion. Reading with students is an effective remedial technique and helps support students as they move into more difficult material.

Accelerated Reader supports all three types of reading practice. When you activate a preference in the software, students are asked if the book they are about to take a quiz on was read to or with them or if they read it independently. This enables you to monitor students' progress with each type of practice.

Reading Ranges for Books Read To and With Students
Generally speaking, books that someone reads *with* a student can be at a little higher level than the books the student reads independently. Books read *to* the student can be a bit more difficult yet. This is because students can readily receive assistance when books are read in tandem or aloud. In addition, listening comprehension is typically better than reading comprehension.

For English language learners, however, this is not always true. Their listening comprehension may be more limited because of a lack of English vocabulary.

Quizzing on Books Read To or With a Student
Make sure students read and quiz in the same way. If a book is read *to* students, the quiz must be read to them as well. In primary-grade classrooms, you may want to enlist parent volunteers or upper-grade students to read books and quizzes to students. (Recorded Voice Quizzes are also available.) If a book is read *with* a student, the quiz must also be read with the student.

Plan a Successful Start

No matter the activity—whether it's exercise, gardening, learning to speak a language, or reading—success is the most effective motivator. Therefore, it's critical that students experience success with their first AR books. Here are some suggestions.

- **For the first AR experience,** read a short, engaging book aloud to the entire class. Make sure the book easily fits the skill level of all students. Project the quiz and take it together.
- **Talk about and model self-monitoring** as a strategy for good comprehension. Tell students to ask themselves, "Am I understanding what I am reading?" If not, advise them to slow down, reread, read ahead, or talk to you or a friend about the confusing part.
- **Teach students how to quiz.** We recommend these strategies:
    - Take the quiz within 24 hours of reading a book.
    - Briefly review the book before you quiz. Retell the story in your head or to a friend, or review the table of contents.
    - Bring your log—not the book—with you to the computer so that you have the exact title or quiz number and can easily locate the quiz in the software.
    - Make sure the quiz title matches the book title.
    - Don't rush through the quiz.
    - Read each question twice and all four answer choices.
    - Paraphrase a question if necessary.

> **Summary**
>
> **GET STUDENTS READING AND QUIZZING**
> - Schedule a regular time for reading practice with self-selected AR books.
> - Plan a successful start by:
>   - Reading a short book aloud and taking the quiz as a class.
>   - Teaching students to monitor their comprehension as they read.
>   - Teaching students how to quiz.

Manage Each Student's Reading Practice

AR gathers data, but you must act on that data if students are to achieve maximum reading growth. We describe here a few strategies for keeping an eye on reading practice and applying thoughtful direction. The most successful AR teachers make these a routine part of their reading practice program.

Have Students Keep a Daily Log

A hand-written log that students maintain enables them to keep track of their reading and allows you to see at a glance how they are spending their time. A log is also motivational. It makes students' reading visual and helps them see how much they have accomplished. AR students are proud of their logs and love to show them to parents and visitors.

Use the Log As a Record of Reading Practice

We have designed logs that you can print from the software, or you can copy one of the reproducible forms that are in the appendix. We show an example of how a log might be filled out on page 27. You can also create your own form. If you devise your own reading log, make sure it includes space for the following information:

- **The student's name and ZPD.** Students must know their ZPD in order to select appropriate books. Having the ZPD on the log also makes it easy for you to see if the books students are reading fall within their ZPD.
- **Information about the book.** This includes the title, quiz number, book level, and point value, and a designation of fiction or nonfiction. Having the quiz number handy helps students locate quizzes in the software. Book level and point value enable you to compare the book's difficulty to the student's ZPD. Knowing whether a book is fiction or nonfiction helps you monitor a student's book choices and determine if one or the other type of literature is harder for the student to read.
- **A record of the student's daily reading.** This includes the date and the number of pages read that day. With this information, you can monitor the pace as well as the frequency of students' practice. High numbers also alert you to students who may be rushing through—or not reading—books because they are focused on earning a large number of points. In the example on page 27, we show one way a student might record how many pages he read in school and out of school: by splitting the box for pages read in half.
- **Personalized point goal.** Having this near at hand reminds students of what they're aiming for. See page 20 for instructions on setting personalized point goals.

Manage Each Student's Reading Practice

Student Reading Log—With Goals

Name: MARTIN LUCERO   ZPD: 4.5-8.0   Class: MRS. SCHEEL

Goals: Average Percent Correct 90% Points 25 Average Book Level 4.5

Quiz No.	Title	Book Level	Points	F/NF	Date	Pages Read Begin - End	Total	Teacher Review/ % Correct	Teacher Notes
8566	THE FOXMAN	4.9	3	F	11/9	1-9	8	✓	
					11/10	10-26 / 27-69	16 / 42	✓	
					11/13	70-86	16		
					11/14	87-109	22	✓	
					11/15	110-119	9	100%	Excellent!
60700	HARRY HOUDINI	6.9	3	NF	11/16	1-18	17	✓	
					11/17	19-31	22		

Reproducible Form, © 2007 Renaissance Learning, Inc.

> **Student Reading Log**
>
> A log helps students keep track of their reading. It also works well as a library pass. If a student shows you his log when he asks to go to the library, you can confirm that he is ready to choose a new book. When the student arrives at the library with his log in hand, the librarian can use the student's ZPD and reading history to help him select another book.

Check in One-on-One at Key Moments

While other programs advocate that teachers should quietly read with students during periods of independent reading, we urge you to be active. Use this time for brief, one-on-one conversations during which you monitor and guide your students' reading practice. This planned and thoughtful guidance is what makes AR different from sustained silent reading. It puts the "guided" in guided independent reading, and is essential to students' reading progress.

Because you are checking each student's "status"—that is, what the student is doing during that particular reading practice period—we call this check-in procedure Status of the Class. To get the most out of AR, take Status of the Class every day. Not only is it the best way to monitor students' practice, it is tremendously motivating. Many students say that having the teacher talk to them routinely about the books they are reading is their favorite part of Accelerated Reader.

Status of the Class Procedure
Establish an efficient monitoring routine to ensure your AR time will be productive. We recommend that you instruct students to have their reading logs filled out and on their desks as they begin reading so it will be easy for you to review them. Begin circulating around the room, but instruct students to interrupt you if they are ready to take a quiz and or have finished a quiz.

Make sure students understand that it's important to take a quiz soon after finishing a book so that the quiz results accurately reflect their comprehension and they can move on to another exciting book.

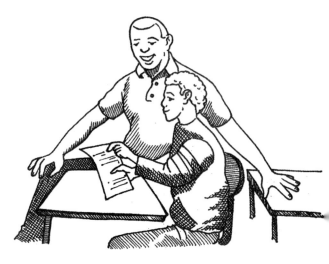

Give students a way to get your attention before and after quizzing that is comfortable for you. Some teachers ask students to simply come up to them and wait quietly. Other teachers prefer that students stay in their seats and raise their hands. Whichever method you choose, emphasize with students that it's important to be quiet and orderly so that classmates can concentrate on their reading.

To maximize reading time, here is a good order in which to meet with students and recommendations for what to do.

First: Students ready to take a quiz. Check the student's reading log to make sure he has indeed read the book he wants to quiz on and his pace seems reasonable. (If a log shows a student has "read" a 1,000-page book overnight, that's a red flag!)

Second: Students who have taken a quiz and are ready to choose their next book. This is the point at which you'll ask yourself, Was the book the student just read too hard or just right? It's also a good time to have a brief conversation with the student about his reading experience and the kind of book he would like to read next.

To help you guide the student to a good choice, AR provides a report called the TOPS Report. It tells you and the student how he did on the quiz he just finished and summarizes what he has accomplished so far in the marking period. If the preference in the software is turned on (which we recommend), a TOPS Report will print automatically after a student finishes a quiz. An example of the TOPS Report is on page 29. Instructions for turning on the preference are in the appendix.

Third: Students who are reading. If a student is just starting a book, check to see if the book level is within the child's ZPD and the interest level and point value are suitable. Ask the student if the book seems like a good fit. Is the book what the student thought it would be? Does it seem too hard or too easy? To help develop comprehension, ask the student what he thinks the book will be about.

If a student is continuing a book she has already started, check the student's reading log to see if she is reading steadily. Ask if she is enjoying her book. Can she give you a brief update on what's happening in the story? What does she think will happen next? Your goal with students as they read is to see if they are having a successful and enjoyable experience, to reinforce comprehension skills, and to motivate them by providing individual attention.

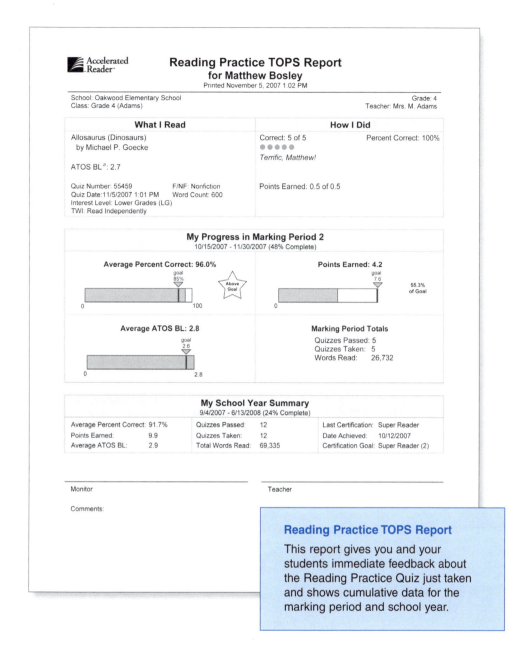

Reading Practice TOPS Report
This report gives you and your students immediate feedback about the Reading Practice Quiz just taken and shows cumulative data for the marking period and school year.

Teaching the TOPS

The TOPS Report is a highly motivational piece of paper. Students love getting immediate and objective feedback. They must be taught how to interpret that feedback, however. Before students begin taking AR quizzes, put an example of the TOPS report on an overhead and go over it as a class. Have students locate and circle the following pieces of information:

- *The number of questions answered correctly.* Very young students may not know what a "percent" is, but can usually understand what "3 out of 5 means," especially if you also show concrete examples. ("The teacher ate 3 out of 5 cookies.")
- *The score on the quiz.* Tell students that this number shows how well they understood what they read. Teach students to aim for scores of 90 percent or

100 percent.
- *Book level.* This indicates how hard the book is. Remind students that, most of the time, the book level must be within their ZPD.
- *The number of points earned.* Explain to students that points tell them how much reading practice they are getting. If you enter point goals in the software, the TOPS Report will show a student's point goal for the marking period. Teach students how to compare the percent of their point goal that they have achieved with the percent of the marking period that has passed. This is a way for them to see whether they are on track to meet their goal.

Use Status of the Class to Promote Self-Directed Learning

When we're pressed for time, we often fall into the habit of telling students what to do because it's faster than waiting for them to think for themselves. But if you use Status of the Class as an opportunity to foster self-directed learning, you will save time in the long run. Students will get better at making their own book choices and at using reading strategies. They will be more efficient, spend more time reading, and comprehend what they read better.

As you meet with students, strive to help them understand themselves and to model the kind of thinking you would like them to take on. Here are suggestions for what language to use.

Instead of Saying …	Say This
"Put this book back. It's too hard for you."	"Why have you chosen this book? Did you notice the book level is higher than your ZPD? Do you still want to read it? What will help you read this successfully?"
"You need to read within your level."	"It's okay to read a few books outside your ZPD, but to get better at reading, most books must be within it. If you read this one, how about we say the next three books must be within your ZPD? If you get high scores, we'll move you into harder books."
"You should be choosing green books, not blue ones."	"I think this book would be a stretch for you, but I know you're really interested in this topic. I could pair you up with Bobby and you could read this together, or you could wait a couple of months. Which would you like to do?"
"I want you to stop reading all these half-point and one-point baby books. Find something worth 2 points."	"Let's find books that will make you stronger as a reader. The other girls are really enjoying _____ . Why don't you take a look at those and the other 2-point books in the reading corner? Pick one, and I'll check in with you every day to see how you're doing."

Review Class Performance at Least Once a Week

Taking Status of the Class, reviewing reading logs, and checking TOPS Reports will help you keep an eye on students' daily work. In addition, we recommend that once a week you look at a summary of each student's overall performance, as well as that of the class as a whole. Doing so will help you spot trends so you can intervene with students who are having trouble.

The Diagnostic Report for Reading Practice Quizzes gives you this information. Take a look at the example below, and you'll see that the report lists every student in the class and notes their average percent correct on AR Reading Practice Quizzes, points earned, and average book level. Notice, too, that the software displays a diagnostic code to alert you to students who likely need your help. Individual goals are also shown, along with each student's progress toward his or her goals. In addition, the report can indicate how much of the student's reading practice has been with fiction, and how much has been done independently. (To have the percent of independent reading displayed on the report, you must turn on a preference. See the appendix for instructions.)

> **If You Don't Print the TOPS Report**
> The TOPS Report is a critical tool for daily monitoring, so if you decide not to print it after every quiz, you need to monitor practice in another way. One option is to instruct students to call you to the computer when they complete a quiz so you can view the results onscreen. Discuss the results and the student's next book choice, record the score on the student's log, and initial it. There are, however, disadvantages: (1) Running back and forth to the computer distracts you from conversations with other students, and (2) by not printing TOPS Reports that you can send home, you lose the chance to communicate with parents. If paper is a problem, try looking for a supply of used office paper that only has printing on one side. Or ask parent groups or businesses to donate money specifically for paper.

We recommend that you review the Diagnostic Report once a week, and that you set the reporting period from the beginning of the marking period to the current date. As you gain experience with AR, you will be able to analyze the Diagnostic Report in depth. However, if you are new to the program, we suggest you focus on a couple of pieces of data: the average percent correct and percent of point goal earned. Confer with each student who has a diagnostic code, analyze the problem, and work together on a solution.

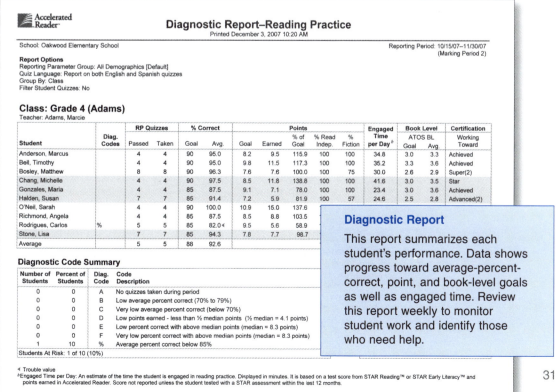

Diagnostic Report
This report summarizes each student's performance. Data shows progress toward average-percent-correct, point, and book-level goals as well as engaged time. Review this report weekly to monitor student work and identify those who need help.

Average Percent Correct Below 85 Percent

The most significant gains in reading ability are associated with high averages on AR quizzes. If a student's average drops below 85 percent, that is a red flag. Below is a chart that lists questions for you to consider when a student's average is low, along with actions to take in response.

Below 85%? Questions to Consider	Actions
• Is the student reading within his ZPD? • Does the student know his ZPD?	• Get the student's suggested ZPD from STAR Reading. Explain what the ZPD means, and have the student record it on his log. (Young students may need to record every number within the range, for example, 1.5, 1.6, 1.7, etc.) Teach the student how to check if a book level is within his ZPD.
• Does the student understand the importance of good comprehension as reflected in high quiz scores, or is he focused on earning points? • Have you and the student established a personalized point goal? When every student has the same goal, many attempt to read more difficult books than they can handle, or rush through books without really understanding them.	• Use the student's GE score on STAR Reading or the student's current ZPD, along with the Goal-Setting Chart on page 73, to set a personalized point goal for each student in the class for the marking period. Be sure to prorate goals on the chart based on how much of the marking period has gone by. For example, if the point goal on the chart is 8.5 and half the marking period has gone by, a reasonable point goal would be 4.2.
• Has the student been reading books within his ZPD but still scoring low?	• Teach the student a simple review strategy, such as reviewing the table of contents or briefly retelling the story to a classmate before quizzing. • If the student still scores low, widen the ZPD to include easier books, and ask the student to select his next few books from this new low end. For example, if the student's current ZPD is 3.0-4.5, widen the ZPD to 2.5-4.5. Help the student find books he is interested in within a book-level range of 2.5-3.0, and watch the quiz results carefully to see how he does.
• Is the student an English language learner struggling with unfamiliar vocabulary and subject matter?	• Help him find books on subjects with which he is familiar. Ask the student to read a page of the book to you. A good rule of thumb is that if a student has problems with five words out of a hundred, the book is too hard. In that case, widen the student's ZPD as described above or help the student select another book with more familiar vocabulary.
• Is the student moving from picture books to chapter books? Is the student choosing very long books and having trouble remembering what he has read? • Does the student need help with comprehension strategies?	• Teach simple comprehension strategies, such as visualization ("make a movie in your head"), previewing before reading, and summarizing after reading. The latter can be done mentally, with a partner, or in a reading journal. Also teach students to slow down or reread when they come to something in a book they don't understand. Check in with these students daily during Status of the Class and help them practice the strategies you teach.

Low Number of Points

Points tell you how much reading a student has successfully completed. As with low quiz averages, there are a number of reasons for a student's point total to be low. To understand the problem, ask yourself the following questions, and then take action.

Low Points? Questions to Consider	Actions
• Has the student been in class for the entire marking period or did she enroll partway through? • Has she been absent frequently?	• Adjust her point goal to reflect her time in school.
• Does the student know how many points she is expected to earn? • Does she have a personalized point goal?	• Establish a personalized point goal as explained above.
• Does she know her ZPD, and is she choosing books within it? Or is she earning few points because her books are too hard and she's doing poorly on quizzes?	• Check to see that the student knows her ZPD and has it with her when she selects books. If she has been scoring low on books within her range, experiment with widening the ZPD by dropping the low end, as described above.
• Is she in the middle of a very long book? The software doesn't "know" that a student has read a book until she takes the quiz.	• Wait to see how the student does on the quiz.
• Is she reading more slowly than average because she is an English language learner?	• Make sure that the books the student is reading are not too hard. If the book level seems okay, lower her point goal to one that is achievable.
• Is the student finding books that interest her? • Does the library have a collection that covers a wide range of subjects at all levels of difficulty?	• Talk with her about her interests. What does she like to do with family? With friends? On her own? Work with the librarian or use the AR search tool on our website to locate titles that match the student's ZPD and interests and are at an appropriate length. Make sure the interest level is suitable for the student's age. • If you have trouble finding suitable books in the school library, talk with your principal and librarian about how to increase the collection.
• Is the student an unmotivated reader?	• AR can help you employ two powerful motivators: good books and success. We have found that if you put the right books in a student's hands and ensure that the student has successful experiences reading and quizzing, that student will be hooked on reading. If you make the student's accomplishments visible to her and celebrate what she has done, she will become more confident, and her motivation and skills will grow.

Keep an Eye on Engaged Time

The Diagnostic Report also shows a calculation called engaged time. This represents the number of minutes per day a student was actively engaged in reading. To calculate this number, we look at the student's GE score on STAR Reading and how many points the student has earned by taking AR quizzes. We compare that to the number of points we can expect the student to earn per minute of reading practice. Then we convert the student's earned points to minutes. For example, let's say Joe Brown has a GE score of 6.5. We know, by consulting the Goal-Setting Chart, that a student of his ability can earn 14 points by reading 30 minutes a day for six weeks. Joe has earned only 7 points. Thus we estimate Joe's engaged time to be only 15 minutes a day. If a student's engaged time is significantly lower than the amount of time you schedule for reading practice, investigate why. It could be that classroom routines are inefficient or books may be hard to access. Since low engaged time is tied to a low number of points earned, see p. 33 for additional causes and remedies.

Summary

MANAGE EACH STUDENT'S READING PRACTICE

- Have students keep a log of daily reading practice.
- Circulate among students every day to check their reading, giving priority to students ready to take a quiz or choose a new book.
- Teach students how to review their TOPS Reports.
- Use interactions with students to promote self-directed learning.
- Review class performance weekly, keeping an eye out for averages below 85 percent, low numbers of points, and low engaged time.

Put Comprehension First

When we examine the reading achievement of students who use AR, we find that those who maintain high scores on quizzes make the most gains. In other words, "just reading" is not enough. Accumulating points is not enough. Students must understand what they are reading, and they must understand it well. The chart below shows the difference in gains made by students in grades 2 through 12 who averaged below 85 percent on AR quizzes and above 85 percent on quizzes.

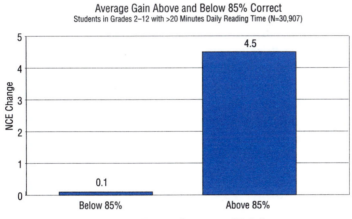

Our data also shows that for students in grades 4 through 12, reading ability improves the most when students average above 90 percent. The chart below summarizes those findings.

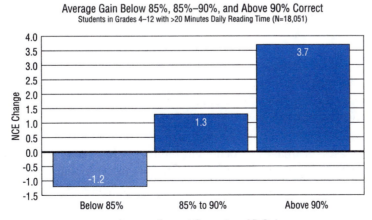

How to Ensure Good Comprehension and High Averages

To achieve high averages, students must score 100 percent on many, if not most, of their AR quizzes. A perfect score indicates that a student understands the key points of a book. It also means the student is reading within a good learning zone. Here are ways to ensure that students reach these high levels of success.

Keep students reading within a range of difficulty that enables them to score 90 or 100 percent on most of their quizzes. Remember that the ZPD suggested by STAR Reading is only a starting place. It is up to you to adjust the range within which students are reading so that they can be successful.

Monitor consistently and in a timely fashion. Take Status of the Class every day. Review recent quiz scores, and check comprehension of the books students are reading. When students take a quiz, have them show you the results right away. Acknowledge good results, probe for the reasons behind not-so-good results, and talk about what kind of book the student might read next.

Explicitly teach comprehension strategies and reinforce them during Status of the Class. Students do not automatically know what to do to help themselves understand text. Research in the field of reading confirms that comprehension strategies must be taught. AR gives students a tremendous opportunity to apply comprehension strategies during independent reading and for you to reinforce them during Status of the Class. There are many books available on good comprehension strategies, but a couple of the most basic are:

- *Self-monitoring.* Model what good readers do when they have trouble understanding a passage. Show how you would slow down, reread, read on, or ask for help. Give students sticky notes and ask them to flag passages they find hard to understand on first reading. When you take Status of the Class, ask students what they did to help themselves overcome the problem.
- *Summarizing.* Tell students that briefly summarizing helps a reader process and remember text. Use the reproducible form on page 75 to make "R.C.W." booklets in which students can periodically jot down a sentence or two about what they've read. (Cut pieces of paper the size of the form; staple the form to the paper as a cover.) Model the strategy and check to see how students are doing with it as you take Status of the Class.

Help students transfer the skills you teach during your instructional period to their AR books. After you teach a reading skill, ask students to apply it during their independent reading time. For example, if you have been teaching the use of context clues, have students identify a word in their AR book that they do not know but can figure out using context clues; as you take Status of the Class, ask students which words, phrases, or images helped them figure out the meaning of the word. If you have been teaching story elements, ask students to think about the central conflict in their book; discuss the conflict briefly as you take Status of the Class.

Teach quiz-taking strategies. Encourage students to pay close attention to AR quizzes. Teach them good quiz-taking strategies, such as reading all the answer choices before selecting one, which will not only help them score well, but will give them practice for other types of tests.

Practices to Avoid

All of us, in our attempts to promote learning, sometimes engage in practices that seem to make sense but are actually ineffective. Fortunately, our research tells us not only what works, but what doesn't work.

Don't Overly Restrict Students' Book Choices
While our research confirms the value of having students read within an individualized zone, it also shows that students can make gains by reading a wide range of books at varying levels of difficulty. This tells us that students can be given a fair amount of freedom to follow their interests. It's okay for them to occasionally read outside their ZPD if they want to relax with an easy book, or if they are eager to tackle a difficult book that really interests them. There is no research to support "stair-stepping" book levels, that is, telling students to read a certain number of books at a specific level before moving on to the next level.

This doesn't mean, however, that it's a good idea for students to read only very short, very easy books when their skills would enable them to read more complex ones. But the best way to move a student into harder books is not to say, "You must read a book at the 4.2 level," but to introduce him to books between, say, the 4.0 and 5.0 levels that you know will interest him, and to teach the student comprehension strategies that will enable him to succeed.

Don't Emphasize Points Over Comprehension
Students tend to think of points in concrete terms. In their minds, it's like money or candy—the more you have, the better. In AR, however, this idea has proven to be too simplistic. Our research shows that when students' averages drop below 80 percent, their reading skills, as measured on standardized tests, can actually decline. This is true no matter how much time they spend reading, or how many points they earn.

> *Summary*
>
> **PUT COMPREHENSION FIRST**
> - Ensure good comprehension by having students read within a range of book levels that enables them to score 90 or 100 percent on most of their quizzes.
> - Monitor student work every day.
> - Teach comprehension strategies and reinforce them during Status of the Class.
> - Teach good quiz-taking strategies.
> - Don't overly restrict students' book choices.
> - Don't emphasize points over comprehension.

Make Success Visible

Whenever we attempt something new or challenging, we need reinforcement to keep going. A dieter needs to see the number on the scale go down. A runner needs to shave a few seconds off his race time. A budding musician needs to be able to play more tunes, more nimbly. No matter what the endeavor, if you find yourself thinking, "I'm not getting anywhere," you're likely to give up.

The same holds true for our students. They can read and read, but if they don't see the progress they're making with reading, they become discouraged or indifferent and resist reading altogether.

Use the Reading Log, Student Record, and TOPS Reports

A reading log, as described earlier, helps students see how much reading they are doing every day and is a concrete reminder of how many books they have read. You can also periodically print a Student Record Report, or students can print the report themselves. This report lists each book a student has read and the student's quiz score. See the example on page below.

The TOPS Report (see page 29) tells the student how she did on the quiz just taken, and thus provides immediate reinforcement for good work. In addition, it shows the student how much progress she has made toward her goals. One of the most important attributes of the TOPS Report is that the student sees it after every quiz. This frequent, objective feedback reinforces effort and keeps students motivated. See the appendix for instructions on how to print the TOPS and Student Record reports.

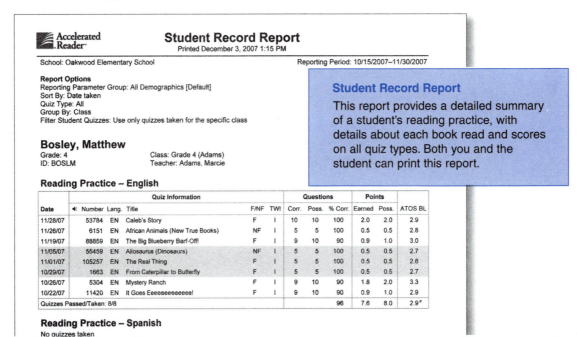

Student Record Report

This report provides a detailed summary of a student's reading practice, with details about each book read and scores on all quiz types. Both you and the student can print this report.

Have Students Chart Their Progress

Some students love to make their progress visual by plotting it on a graph. An example of a simple graph that students can use to keep track of how close they are to achieving an average of 90 percent on AR quizzes is shown below. An example of a graph for showing progress toward an individualized point goal is below (Reproducible forms are in the appendix.) Give students the data they need for their charts when you run your weekly Diagnostic Report. Some teachers do this verbally as they take Status of the Class; others slice the Diagnostic Report into pieces with a paper cutter and give each student his or her line of data.

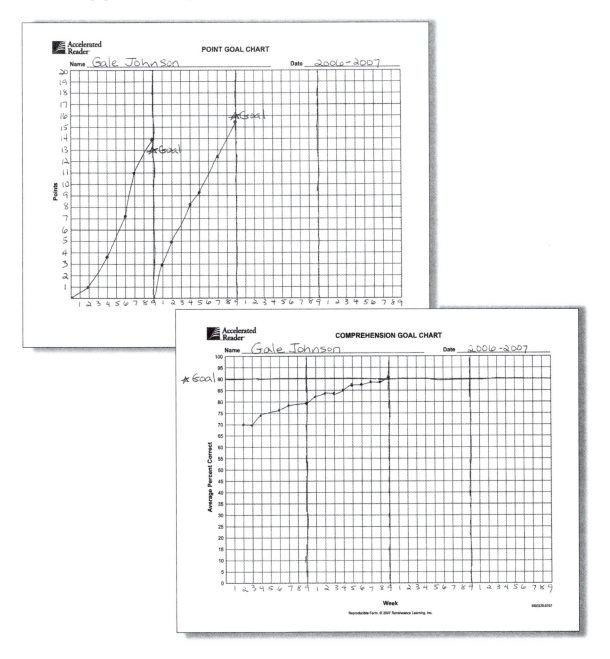

Have Students "Collect" Success

Give students a sheet of paper divided into squares like a Bingo chart. Every time a student scores 90 or 100 percent on a quiz, give her a sticker to put in one of the squares. Let students know that when the chart is full, they will get a prize. A book makes for a great prize! Some teachers acquire a collection of free books from book orders and let students choose which one they want.

Create a Class Bulletin Board

Effective AR teachers establish a special place in their classroom where they display and celebrate student achievement. The best visuals show progress toward individual goals. For point goals, divide a bulletin board into four sections: 25% of Goal, 50% of Goal, 75% of Goal, and 100% of Goal.

When 25 percent of the marking period has gone by, list the names of the students who have achieved 25 percent of their point goal in the "25% of Goal" section. When 50 percent of the marking period has gone by, move the names of the students who have reached 50 percent of their point goal to this section, and so on. Many teachers use a theme for this display, such as "Reading Rockets" or "Reading Stars."

You can also establish a "90 Percent Club." List the names of students who achieve an average of at least 90 percent on AR quizzes and update the list weekly.

Establish a School Display

Many schools highlight student achievement with a "Reading Wall of Fame." This is displayed prominently in a central area where it will draw the attention of students, parents, and visitors. Like the classroom bulletin board described above, it celebrates the work of students who meet their individual goals and frequently is based on a schoolwide theme. Often, the accomplishments of the entire school are also emphasized: the total number of books or words read, for example, or the percentage of students schoolwide who have an average greater than 85 or 90 percent on AR quizzes.

Introduce Students and Parents to Renaissance Home Connect

If you have the Renaissance Place Enterprise version of Accelerated Reader, your students are able to view their daily progress from any computer with Internet access using a feature called Renaissance Home Connect. Students can also see all the books they've read so far and find new books to read. Through Renaissance Home Connect, parents and guardians can share and reinforce their children's success and thus help keep them motivated. Parents also have the option to receive email notifications at home or at work when their child has completed an AR quiz. Renaissance Home Connect is easy for teachers to initiate: You need only generate informational letters from the software. (See the appendix for instructions.) These are individualized and include the web address along with login information for the student and his or her parents.

Summary

MAKE SUCCESS VISIBLE

- Use the reading log and the Student Record and TOPS reports to make success visible to students.
- Have students chart their progress.
- Create class bulletin boards and school displays that highlight achievements.
- Facilitate the use of Renaissance Home Connect so that parents can share in their children's accomplishments.

Spread the Joy of Reading

Books are magical. They have the power to teach, to move, and to enthrall. They transport us to faraway places, ignite our imaginations, and challenge our minds. However, many students in our classrooms have never had these experiences. They rarely choose to read, and when they do, it is unrewarding, either because reading is too hard or because it does not invoke an emotional or intellectual response.

The fundamental mission of Accelerated Reader is to bring the joy of reading to every student. We have seen, over and over again, that once students experience the magic of reading, they willingly and happily read. In fact, you can't stop them from reading, and their reading skills grow dramatically. That's why, at its heart, AR is not about the quizzes, the points, or the technology. It's about turning kids on to books.

Reading to Students

There is no better way to acquaint students with the pleasures of reading than to read to them, and we recommend you do that regularly. For primary-grade students, listening to books read aloud is, of course, one of the beginning steps in learning to read, but even high-school students love this activity.

When you read aloud to students, you introduce them to books they might not yet be able to read independently, expose them to new genres and authors, and build their desire to enhance their skills. Good books "sell" reading.

Reading aloud also enables you to teach and model comprehension strategies, such as visualizing, making predictions, previewing, questioning, clarifying, and summarizing. It also presents good opportunities for class discussions on vocabulary, characterization, plot, and other literary elements.

Book Talks

Informal book talks are a fun way to pique students' interest in books. Pick out a few titles that you know are popular, hold up or display them, and say a few things about each book aimed at enticing students to read it. You might read the first few sentences or pages if the beginning is particularly compelling. Your librarian can help you find suitable titles, but students will be even more interested if you have read the books yourself and can recommend them.

Book Discussions and Literature Circles

Whole-class and small-group discussions about favorite books and authors promote a reading culture. Discussions can be formal activities (students give presentations on their favorite authors) or informal—a conversation among students who have read the same book, for example. The most effective ones emphasize reflection and personal response. Sometimes teachers give students sticky notes to mark passages they particularly like or find surprising, confusing, or funny. Another strategy is to give students prompts that will jump-start discussion, such as, "If I were this character, I would …," "I liked the part where …," or "I wonder ….."

Finding the Right Book with AR BookFinder

A surefire way to turn a student on to reading is to introduce him to just the right book. AR BookFinder is a free online tool designed to help you do that. With it, students, parents, teachers, or librarians can:

- Search for books that have a corresponding AR quiz by using such criteria as book level, interest level, title, author, and/or subject.
- Search for collections like ALA Notables, state lists for all fifty states, and librarians' picks.
- View details about specific books, including a summary, ATOS level, interest level, word and page counts, book covers, and ISBNs.
- Create a list of books and print it.

AR BookFinder helps students—either on their own or with the assistance of parents, teachers, and librarians—identify books that match their interests, maturity level, and ZPD. They can then bring a list of those titles to the school library, public library, or bookstore. In addition, parents can find titles for gifts or reading aloud to their children. Teachers can quickly view details that help them see if a book is suitable for an individual student or for reading to their class. In addition, teachers who have BookGuide, which is a separate software program, can create book lists that students and parents can access through BookFinder. To use AR BookFinder, go to www.arbookfind.com.

Summary

SPREAD THE JOY OF READING

- "Sell" reading to students by reading good books aloud.
- Introduce students to interesting books through informal book talks.
- Organize small-group discussions and literature circles in which students can share personal responses to books.
- Use AR BookFinder to help match students and books.

Managing AR in Your Classroom

Student Routines and Responsibilities

When AR is implemented effectively, there's a lot going on at once. Students are reading, quizzing, and selecting books. You are reviewing logs and reports, guiding book selection, and keeping an eye on students taking quizzes. Efficient student routines not only maximize reading practice time, they keep you from feeling overwhelmed. Just be sure to demonstrate the routines thoroughly, and anticipate a period during which you will need to give students feedback—individually and as a class—on how they're doing. Post the rules, reteach or adjust routines as needed, and don't forget to celebrate when everything goes well.

Reading Folders

Give every student a folder in which to keep his or her Accelerated Reader paperwork. This includes:

- Student Reading Log
- TOPS Reports
- Any motivational charts or graphs that students use

If students are in the same classroom all day, pass out AR folders (or have a helper pass them out) as part of the morning routine. That way, no minutes are wasted when AR time comes around.

Alternatively, instead of passing folders out every morning, have students keep their folders in a certain corner of their desk. (Even if you have multiple classes throughout the day, students can still keep folders in the desks. Use folders of different colors for different classes.) Students can log any additional reading they do outside of AR time—when they're finished with an assignment, for example.

Reading Practice

Emphasize with students that AR time is a time for reading quietly. Teach students the following routine:

1. Get out your reading log and AR book.
2. Record the beginning page for the day's reading on the log, and leave the log open on your desk. (If students are reading somewhere else in the room, instruct them to have their logs with them.)
3. Read and enjoy your book.
4. When AR time is over, write down the number of the page where you stopped, put your log back in your AR folder, and put the folder away.

Some teachers like to signal the start of AR time by having students do a special AR chant. Other teachers say something like, "It's AR time. You have one minute to sit down, get your folder out, jot down the date and page, and get your nose in your book." If the teacher sees a student is not settling down, she approaches the student quietly and gives a gentle warning, "Jill, 15 seconds left." After awhile, the teacher need only say, "It's AR time," and students know what to do.

Taking Quizzes

Students must follow an established procedure before taking a quiz. You want to make sure that students have read the books they want to quiz on, and have equal and timely access to computers. The routine that you set up will depend on how many computers you have in your room and whether there is typically a wait time to use them. In lower-grade classrooms, for example, computers are usually in heavy demand since beginning readers tend to read many short books.

- Instruct students to come to you before quizzing and show you their reading log. You review the student's reading history with the book he's ready to quiz on and check to see if it's reasonable. If the student must go out of the room to quiz, initial the log or otherwise indicate on the log that it's okay for him to take a quiz. Tell students that they must not take the book with them when they quiz, just their log.
- If students are quizzing in your room, develop a system for using the computer. Some teachers ask students to write their name in a special area on the board. After a student quizzes, she erases her name, and the next person on the list can go to the computer. Or you could do the following:
    1. Students decorate their folders so they are easily identified. They also write their name in large letters on the front.
    2. When ready to quiz, a student shows you his log. You give the student permission to take a quiz, and the student places his folder at the bottom of a stack next to the computer.
    3. You keep your eye on the stack, and let a student know when his folder reaches the top. Students also have permission to tap the next person on the shoulder if you are busy.

4. If a student has time during another part of the day—after finishing an assignment, for example—and you see his folder at the top of the stack, send him to the computer to quiz.
- After a student quizzes, he brings his TOPS Report to you. You immediately review the quiz results with the student, sign the report, and briefly discuss his next book choice.
- The student records the quiz results on his reading log, and puts the TOPS Report in his folder.
- He selects his next book right away, or as soon as possible.

Quizzing with NEO 2 Laptops

If your students take quizzes on NEO 2 laptops instead of full-sized computers, you may need to adjust your quizzing routines. Be aware, first of all, that TOPS Reports will print on whichever printer is connected to the computer with which you manage AR. We strongly recommend that this printer be situated inside your classroom so that students can retrieve TOPS Reports immediately. In addition, make sure that students have a quiet environment in which to take quizzes. If students use NEO 2s at their desks, you can create a screen out of two folders that they can put around them to minimize distractions. Alternatively, you can create a special quizzing area in your room, and students can bring their NEO 2s there to quiz. For instructions on logging in and taking a quiz on the NEO 2, see page 70.

Taking TOPS Reports Home

Besides providing the student with instant feedback, the TOPS Report is a communication tool between school and home. We recommend that TOPS Reports be sent home in a separate school-to-home folder—not the AR folder—that may contain other student work for parents to see. (Some teachers send work home daily; others do it once a week.) The reports don't need to come back. You can access the data they contain from other AR reports.

Summary

STUDENT ROUTINES AND RESPONSIBILITIES
- Give students folders in which to keep AR materials.
- Teach students efficient routines for reading quietly and taking quizzes.
- Send TOPS Reports to parents in a school-to-home folder.

Teacher Routines

It's important that you develop efficient routines, along with your students. When procedures become habits, you have more time to monitor and help your students.

Interacting with Students

Taking Status of the Class during AR time is your most important routine. Don't plan any other activity—no grading of tests, for example, or other paperwork. If you are quick and efficient, you can get to 25 students in half an hour. It may take time, however, to build up this competency! In the meantime, we suggest you use the Status of the Class Record Sheet that is in the appendix. If you keep track of the students you see every day, you will be sure no one is neglected. Even good readers benefit from a few words of support every couple of days.

Running Reports and Reviewing Data

Pick a day on which you will run the Diagnostic Report each week. Many teachers choose Fridays. Look to see which students have an average below 85 percent or a diagnostic code. Highlight their names, and talk to them first on the following Monday during Status of the Class. Check off their names as you speak with them. Some teachers take notes on the Diagnostic Report and save the report in their gradebook until the end of the marking period.

In addition, many teachers view the Diagnostic Report onscreen every day, either just before or after AR time. Have any diagnostic codes popped up? Have any averages fallen? This is not a substitute for Status of the Class, but an additional way to closely monitor students' day-to-day work.

Alternatively, if you have the Renaissance Place version of AR, you can look at the Class Record Book onscreen every day before taking Status of the Class. This screen also alerts you to students having trouble.

Celebrating Success

Regular acknowledgment of work well done is a good routine to get into. Consistent reinforcement is not only fair and motivating, it teaches students to recognize their own success. Whatever you do to celebrate achievement, make sure it takes into account individual differences and goals, and does not create competitive situations in which only the more able readers are praised.

Acknowledge Quiz Scores of 100 Percent

High scores on quizzes are associated with the greatest reading gains. Reinforce perfect scores with one of the following, or any other small acknowledgment:

- A jellybean or other small treat from a jar next to the computer
- A pass that allows the student to skip a homework assignment of the student's choice
- The opportunity to be first in line for an activity

Recognize Progress Toward Goals

Meeting an individual goal is a reason to celebrate. In addition to the charts and bulletin boards described on pages 39 and 40, consider other routines, like the following:

- Give certificates or blue ribbons to students who averaged at least 85 percent and met their point goal for the marking period. Add an extra acknowledgment for students who averaged 90 percent or higher.
- Send to each student's home a blank envelope with the child's name on it. Ask parents to write a letter of congratulations for making AR goals that also includes a special incentive, such as playing a game or going to a movie alone with Mom or Dad. Have parents put the letter into the envelope, seal it, and return it to school. Hang the envelopes in the classroom. When a student meets his individual goals, he opens the envelope.

Summary

TEACHER ROUTINES AND RESPONSIBILITIES

- Interact with students every day.
- Review data at least once a week with the Diagnostic Report and/or the Class Record Book.
- Acknowledge quiz scores of 100 percent.
- Recognize progress toward individual goals.

Common Questions

Reading is a complex task and students are complicated human beings. Whether you're new to AR or have years of experience, questions will come up! Here are some of the ones that we are asked most often in our seminars and webinars.

Our school can't afford STAR Reading, at least not this year. Can we still use AR?
Yes. You just need to have another method in place for identifying an initial ZPD for each student. To do that, you can use a grade-equivalent score from any standardized test and then refer to the Goal-Setting Chart on p. 76 to find the corresponding ZPD. If a standardized test is not available, use your professional judgment and start each student in a range of book levels that seems about right. Once the student starts taking AR Reading Practice Quizzes, you can adjust the initial ZPD up or down until you see the student is able to score above 80 percent on a quiz and maintain a quiz average of at least 85 percent.

Our parents think it's unfair for every student in a class to have a different point goal. What should we tell them?
You might make a comparison to athletics. Would it be fair for every student of the same age to practice football at the same level of intensity regardless of ability? Like running, tackling, and throwing a ball, reading is a skill. The only way for an individual to make progress is to practice at a level that is appropriate. Point out to parents that individualized goals level the playing field and give every student an equal chance at success.

Why do you say that students must not bring their book to the computer when they quiz? Isn't "looking back" a comprehension strategy that all readers must learn and apply?
Being aware that you don't understand what you're reading and paging back to bolster your comprehension is indeed an important strategy. It is one that students must learn to use while they are reading. In addition, referring back to a passage to find the answer to a question is an essential technique for taking a high-stakes test. However, taking an AR quiz is a different situation. It is an assessment of general comprehension of a book as a whole. If students look up answers while they take an AR quiz, the only thing that is assessed is their ability to look up answers. The better instructional approach is to encourage students to look back whenever they are unsure of what is going on in their book as they are reading it. When students are finished with a book, they can also do a self-check and see if they can recall the important characters and events. They can review the book again if they have to.

After they have finished this review, then they can go to the computer—without the book—and take the AR quiz. This method reinforces looking back as a metacognitive skill, that is, a skill students use to think about their thinking, not to answer specific test questions.

I'm concerned that if I emphasize maintaining a high average—85 or 90 percent—on AR quizzes, students will only read super-easy books. Some students might even purposefully make mistakes on their STAR tests in order to lower their ZPDs. Isn't it better to push students into harder and harder books even if they only average 75 percent?

Even though it might seem like common sense to challenge students in this way, our research on independent reading practice does not support this practice. High comprehension is associated with reading growth; low comprehension is not. At the same time, we do want students to read within a range suitable for their actual reading ability, and we want students to ultimately be able to read complex, sophisticated material. Here are a few things to keep in mind:

1. Introduce students to challenging text with instructional materials during your instructional reading period. Teach the strategies they need to be successful. Scaffold their efforts with prereading activities and discussion.
2. Keep the focus during AR time on independent recreational practice. Remember that one of AR's biggest goals is to foster a love of reading. Acquaint students with popular and engaging books by reading aloud to your class and helping individuals select books in the library. If students follow their interests, they will naturally choose books throughout their ZPD. As a student's ability grows, widen the ZPD by raising the higher end.

Sometimes a student wants to read outside his ZPD. Is that okay?

Yes. If students are selecting books based on their interests, they may occasionally want to read one that is below or above their ZPD. If the book looks difficult, you might pair the student up with someone who will read the book with him. We also recommend you check in with the student regularly to see how he's doing. If the student routinely selects books outside his ZPD, make sure he knows what his ZPD is and what it means. Probe to find out why he's making these choices. You might make a bargain with the student: He must read a certain number of books within his ZPD before reading one outside of it.

If a student does poorly on a quiz, should she retake it the next day and try to improve her score?

No. A low quiz score signals a need for diagnosis and intervention. Was the book within the student's ZPD? Did she actually read it? Is it noted on her reading log? Is the ZPD appropriate? Does the book have a specialized vocabulary that would make it particularly difficult for this student? Figure out what went wrong and then help the student have a successful experience with her next book.

I didn't know about interest levels until reading this book! Where do I find this information?

To find the interest level for a specific book, go to either www.arbookfind.com or our online Quiz Store (www.renlearn.com) and type in the title. If you have the Renaissance Place version of Accelerated Reader, you can also view book information through the software. From the Home page, scroll to the Accelerated Reader tab and click Manage Quizzes. Click Reading Practice. Locate the book for which you want information and click Select.

I teach first grade, and most of my students can't read on their own. Can I use AR?
Definitely. But an AR classroom with emergent and beginning readers looks somewhat different than one that consists entirely of established readers. See p. 88 for tips on using AR with primary students.

I'm a high school principal. Our teachers have a lot of content to cover and not much scheduling flexibility. How can we fit in AR?
There are a number of approaches. One is to tweak your existing school schedule: Take a few minutes out of each class and/or shorten the passing time between classes to create a separate 20-minute AR period each day. Alternatively, you could turn existing homeroom or advisor time into AR time. A third option is to have content teachers take turns providing reading practice; in some high schools, for example, reading practice takes place during math on Mondays, during history on Tuesdays, and so on. Sometimes the most successful approach is to recreate the schedule by first establishing a whole-school reading practice period (often first thing in the morning) and then rebuilding the school day. Whichever approach you take, inspire the support and participation of all staff, provide professional development, and carve out a minimum of 20 minutes each day—research shows that less than that is ineffective.

When You're Ready To Do More

Set Additional Goals

AR enables you to enter three goals in the software for each student. We've already discussed the importance of making the point goal a personalized goal related to a student's reading ability, and we've described how to set reasonable point goals using the Goal-Setting Chart. (See page 76.) In addition, you can set goals for average percent correct and average book level. When you enter these goals in the computer, you set them for a marking period. The software will then show each student's progress toward goals on the TOPS, Diagnostic, and Goal History reports.

Average-Percent-Correct Goal

The minimum goal for all students must be 85 percent. Ninety percent is an even better goal. However, students might not be able to reach this higher average until they are used to taking quizzes and have incorporated comprehension strategies. So that students don't get discouraged, you may want to initially set average-percent-correct goals at 85. When students have met that goal, you can slowly raise it. The software allows you to set a goal for individual students at any value from 85 to 90 percent.

Book-Level Goal

The purpose of this goal is to ensure students read at a level appropriate for them as individuals. While it's tempting to set the same goal for every student—6.0 for sixth-graders, for example—our research tells us that this is not an effective practice. Nor does research support challenging students by continuously raising their book-level goals by .1 increments.

What research does show is that wide reading of books that students enjoy and can comfortably read leads to the greatest gains. For this reason, we recommend you set a book-level goal in the following way:

1. Using the Goal-Setting Chart on page 76, find the ZPD that correlates to a student's GE score on STAR Reading or another standardized test. (If you use Lexiles, consult the Goal-Setting Chart for ATOS 2000, which is on p. 77.)
2. Set the book-level goal at the low end of the ZPD. For example, if a student's GE is 6.0 and her ZPD is 4.0 to 6.1, set her book-level goal at 4.0.
3. Encourage the student to read throughout her ZPD. Her average book level will then exceed her goal.

If a student only reads books at the low end of her ZPD and you feel she is capable of reading harder books, we recommend that you not raise the book-level goal. Instead, set a separate goal with the student to read one or two books during the marking period that are at the higher end of her ZPD.

Book-Level Goal and Additional STAR Tests
You may test students with STAR Reading a number of times during the school year to check progress. If you do, two questions may come up: When a student's GE score goes up on a STAR Reading assessment, should the ZPD and book-level goal be raised? If the STAR assessment reports a lower GE (which can happen if tests are given frequently, due to the standard error of measurement), should the ZPD and book-level goal be lowered?

The answer to both questions is not necessarily. Think back to our analogy of working with a personal trainer. The best indicator of fitness is what you are able to do in your daily workout. The best indicator of what a student is able to read is how the student does with daily reading, as measured by AR quizzes. If a new STAR test prompts you to take a look at students' ZPDs and goals, that's fine. But base any adjustments you make on a student's performance with AR.

Set Goals *with* Students, Not *for* Students

Setting goals with students is one of the most powerful components of Accelerated Reader. Goals must not be imposed upon students, however, but developed with them. When you establish goals with students, you give them the opportunity to reflect upon their abilities and what they want to achieve. As a result, they "own" their goals and feel a sense of control and purpose.

Students will need a record of their goals so that they don't forget them. Have students write their goals on their reading log and keep the log in their AR folder.

Here is a simple goal-setting process:

1. Meet briefly with each student at the beginning of each marking period. Have the student's GE score from STAR Reading and the Goal-Setting Chart. If you are partway through the school year, also have a copy of the student's Student Record Report so you can see what the student has done so far.
2. Have a conversation with the student, and decide on personalized, realistic goals. Record the goals and give the student a copy.
3. Enter the goals into the software. See the appendix for instructions.

Don't Be Afraid to Adjust Goals

Setting appropriate goals is more of an art than a science. Always use your best judgment, staying with or deviating from the suggestions on the Goal-Setting Chart as needed. The important thing is that goals be personal and attainable. As you set them, balance the need to encourage effort and achieve growth with the need to keep your students' reading experiences successful and pleasurable. If a goal proves unattainable despite a student's best efforts, adjust it, even in the middle of a marking period.

Become a Model Classroom, Library, or School

One of the best ways to get the most from Accelerated Reader is to enroll in our certification program. Certification marks you as a skilled professional who understands and implements best practices. It lets you—and the rest of the world—know that you are doing things right. Certification is also a great way to focus your students' energy and help them achieve even greater gains.

You can certify as a model classroom, library, or school by meeting a set of criteria that are based on the best practices outlined in this book. Once you certify, we'll acknowledge your efforts with awards, discounts, and professional recognition. You'll also have the opportunity to share your knowledge with teachers across the nation at our symposia.

For more information about the program, visit our website and click the Renaissance Certification link.

Summary

SET ADDITIONAL GOALS

- Set individual goals for book level and average percent correct, as well as for points.
- Set goals with students, not for students.
- Adjust goals anytime to keep students' reading experiences successful and pleasurable.
- Aim to certify as a model classroom, library, or school.

Enhance Practice and Analyze Data More Deeply

Accelerated Reader software contains features, quizzes, and reports that can help you monitor many forms of reading practice and various types of reading skills. Most of these are available with every version of AR; a few, such as Vocabulary and Literacy Skills quizzes may need to be purchased separately. The most critical resource, however, is not part of the software at all—that is, books.

Expand Your Book Collection

Book circulation rises at least fourfold in the first year and often more. As students get excited about reading, you'll find yourself needing more books, at more levels, to suit more varied interests. It's a great problem to have, and one you must solve in order to keep students involved and excited.

Here are some ideas for securing more books for your library and/or classroom collection:

- **Pick up books at garage sales** and thrift stores. Become a book scavenger!
- **If parents ordinarily give you a holiday gift**, ask them to donate a book instead.
- **Talk to the school's parent group** about sponsoring a bake sale or other fundraising activity.
- **Send letters to local businesses** and service groups asking for books or cash.
- **Launch a book drive.** Let everyone know you need books and provide a list of the ones you'd like. Set a goal, come up with a theme, and keep the media informed of progress. Hold a ceremony when you meet your goal, and invite all the benefactors.

Utilize Other AR Reports

AR includes more than 40 reports. Of these, the TOPS and Diagnostic Reports are the most important ones to view regularly. Below we describe two other reports—the Student Record Report and the TWI Report—that will help you monitor student data. But don't hesitate to explore the other reports available. See the appendix for instructions on viewing and printing them.

Student Record Report
This report summarizes a student's reading activity for any period of time that you indicate—one week, a marking period, or an entire school year, for example. It lists

book titles, their reading level and point value, and quiz scores. It also summarizes data, giving the average reading level of books read and the average score on quizzes, and calculates the number of points earned. An example is on page 38.

The Student Record Report is invaluable for diagnosing problems. If a student has a diagnostic code on the Diagnostic Report, for example, you can view the Student Record Report to analyze details about the student's reading activity. Ask yourself:

- Were the books the student chose to read within her ZPD?
- Did the student do well with books of a certain level and poorly with others?
- Did the student do well with books of a certain length, as indicated by point value, and poorly with others?
- Is the student struggling with either fiction or nonfiction?

TWI Report

If you have students taking quizzes on books that someone has read to or with them, you will find the TWI Report useful. It tells you how each student is doing with these two kinds of reading practice, as well as with independent reading. In order for you to generate a TWI Report, however, someone with administrator access must turn on the TWI setting in the preferences section of the software before students begin taking quizzes. Then, when students select a quiz to take, the software will ask them if the book was read to or with them, or if they read it independently. An example of a TWI Report is below.

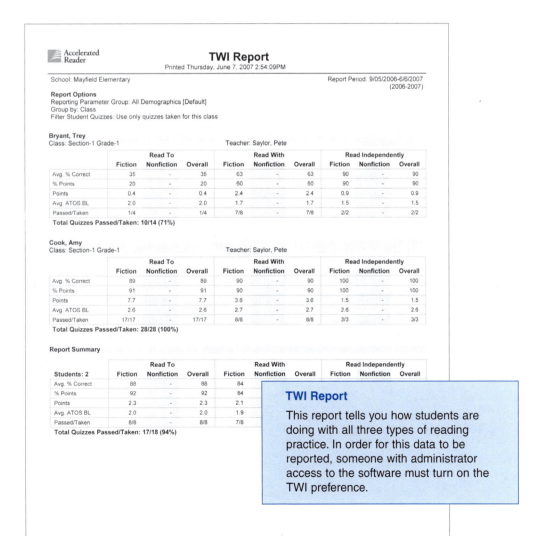

TWI Report

This report tells you how students are doing with all three types of reading practice. In order for this data to be reported, someone with administrator access to the software must turn on the TWI preference.

Use Other AR Quizzes

With Accelerated Reader, you can assess more than reading practice. We have developed additional quizzes that provide data on vocabulary acquisition, literacy skills, and comprehension of specific textbook series. If you have the Enterprise edition of AR, most of these quizzes are automatically available to you. Otherwise, you can purchase them through our website. Below is a description of each type. For more information on how to best use the quizzes with students, sign up for one of our professional-development offerings.

Vocabulary Practice Quizzes
Vocabulary Practice Quizzes reinforce key vocabulary words in the books students choose for independent reading. This ensures that words for study are personalized and meaningful. The process goes like this: The student selects a book within his ZPD that he is interested in reading as part of his on-going reading practice. He or the teacher prints a vocabulary list for the book from the AR software. The list includes 5, 10, or 15 words, depending on the difficulty of the book and the richness of its vocabulary. The student reads the book and reviews the words. After taking and passing the Reading Practice Quiz, the student takes the Vocabulary Practice Quiz. A TOPS Report gives the student and teacher immediate feedback on how the student did.

Literacy Skills Quizzes
Literacy Skills Quizzes help you measure your students' proficiency with 24 higher-level reading and critical-thinking skills. They are available for many of the most popular books in the AR database. Most quizzes have 12 questions, drawn from a bank of 36 questions. Each quiz comes with an electronic teacher's guide that contains a brief summary of the book, discussion questions, and extension activities. Some teachers use Literacy Skills Quizzes with whole-class novels to prepare students for high-stakes tests. Other teachers have students take quizzes on books they are reading independently so they can monitor comprehension skills and plan instruction.

Other Reading Quizzes
Other Reading Quizzes enable you to check comprehension of material that students read in specific textbook series. The process goes like this: You teach a lesson as you normally would from the basal reader or textbook and assign the reading suggested by the teacher's guide. Students take an Other Reading Quiz, which checks literal comprehension. You can then view AR reports to plan what to do next. Data is reported for individual students so that you can group students or work with individuals who need extra help. Quizzes are aligned to selections in pupil anthologies, big books, phonics readers, and other materials, and are available for such series as Harcourt's *Trophies*, Scott Foresman's *Reading Street* and *Lectura*, SRA McGraw-Hill's *Open Court*, and MacMillan/McGraw-Hill's *Treasures*. See our website for a complete list.

> **Summary**
>
> **ENHANCE PRACTICE AND ANALYZE DATA MORE DEEPLY**
>
> - Expand your book collection so that students have plenty of books from which to choose.
> - Use the Student Record and TWI reports to analyze the work of individual students.
> - Monitor growth in additional reading skills with Vocabulary Practice, Literacy Skills, and Other Reading Quizzes.

Appendix

Instructions for Common Software Tasks
Renaissance Place Version

Using STAR Assessments

Log Into STAR Reading as a Teacher/Administrator, Locate Pretest Instructions, and Enter a Monitor Password
1. On the Welcome page, click **Teacher/Administrator**.
2. Enter your user name and password.
3. On the Renaissance Place Home Page, scroll to STAR Reading and click **Resources**. Click **Pretest Instructions**.
4. Close and click **Home**. Scroll to STAR Reading. Click **Preferences**. Click **Set Monitor** and enter a monitor password. Click **Save**.

Log Into STAR Early Literacy as a Teacher/Administrator, Select Testing Options, and Enter a Monitor Password
1. On the Welcome page, click **Teacher/Administrator**.
2. Enter your user name and password.
3. On the Renaissance Place Home Page, scroll to STAR Early Literacy and click **Preferences**. Click **Testing Options**. Select options and click **Save**.
4. Click **Testing Password**. Click the box next to Monitor and enter a monitor password. Click **Save Selection**.

Identify Students' User Names and Passwords
1. On the Renaissance Place Home Page, scroll to STAR Reading or STAR Early Literacy and click **Reports**.
2. Under Other Reports, select **Student Information.**
3. Select options and click **View Report**. Click **Print**.

Log Into STAR Reading or STAR Early Literacy as a Student and Take a Test
1. On the Welcome page, click **Student**.
2. Enter a user name and password.
3. Under STAR Reading, click **Take a Test**.
4. Click **Start**. Enter a monitor password if required.
5. Abort the test with **Ctrl A** (Windows) or **Open Apple A** (Macintosh).

View and Customize STAR Reports
1. On the Renaissance Place Home Page, scroll to STAR Reading and click **Reports**.
2. Click the name of the report you wish to view or print.
3. Select options and click **View Report**. Click **Print**.

Getting Results with Accelerated Reader

Working With AR Reading Practice Quizzes

Identify Students' User Names and Passwords
1. On the Renaissance Place Home Page, scroll to Accelerated Reader and click **Reports**.
2. Click **School Management**. Click **Student Information**.
3. Select options and click **View Report**. Click **Print**.

Log Into Accelerated Reader as a Student and Take a Reading Practice Quiz
1. On the Welcome page, click **Student**. Enter a user name and password. Click **Login**.
2. Under Accelerated Reader, click **Take a Quiz**.
3. Click **Take a Reading Practice Quiz**.
4. Enter a title and click **Search**.
5. Click the quiz title. If you are asked how you read the book, click on your answer. On the Confirm Quiz page, click **Yes**.
6. Abort the quiz with **Escape**.

Edit Quiz Information and Preview a Quiz
1. On the Renaissance Place Home page, scroll to Accelerated Reader and click **Manage Quizzes**.
2. Click **Reading Practice**.
3. Type in a quiz title and click **Search**.
4. Click **Select**.
5. Click **Edit Select Quiz Information**.
6. Edit and click **Save**.
7. Return to quiz list by clicking **Reading Practice** at the top of the screen.
8. Choose a title, search by book level, or click **More Criteria** to search by point value, fiction or nonfiction, interest level, or language. Click **Select**.
9. Click **Take a Sample Quiz**.
10. Click **Start Quiz**.

Set the Automatic Student Logout
1. On the Renaissance Place Home page, scroll to Accelerated Reader and click **Preferences**.
2. Under Classroom Preferences, click **Student Quizzing**.
3. Click **Edit Student Quizzing**.
4. Click the box next to Automatic Student Logout to check it.
5. Click **Save**.

Edit TWI Settings
Those with administrator access:
1. On the Renaissance Place Home page, scroll to Accelerated Reader and click **Preferences**.
2. Under School Preferences, click **Student Quizzing**.
3. Click **Edit Student Quizzing**.
4. Scroll to **TWI Monitoring** and click the box to check or remove a check.
5. Click **Save**.

Those with teacher access (an administrator must enable TWI Monitoring for the school before you can adjust the setting for your class):
1. On the Renaissance Place Home page, scroll to Accelerated Reader and click **Preferences**.
2. Under Classroom Preferences, click **Individual Student Settings**.
3. Click **Edit TWI Settings**.
4. Use the drop-down list in the row for each student to choose a setting. To apply the same setting to all students, click the **TWI Settings** drop-down list and choose a setting. Click **Update all students**.
5. Click **Save**.

Setting Goals

Select a Marking Period
1. On the Renaissance Place Home page, scroll to Accelerated Reader and click **Class Record Books**.
2. Click **Reading Practice Goals**.
3. Click **Select Marking Periods**.
4. Under Available School Marking Periods, click **Select** for the marking period you would like to use.
5. Click **Save**.

Enter Student Goals
1. On the Renaissance Place Home page, scroll to Accelerated Reader and click **Class Record Books**.
2. Click **Reading Practice Goals**.
3. On the View Reading Practice Goals Record Book, click **Edit Student Goals**.
4. Enter goals.
5. Click **Save**.

Viewing Quiz Data and Printing Reports

View Data with the Class Record Book
1. On the Renaissance Place Home page, scroll to Accelerated Reader and click **Class Record Books**.
2. Click **Reading Practice Quizzes**.
3. Click a student's name to view quiz data.

Locate, View, and Print Reports
1. On the Renaissance Place Home page, scroll to Accelerated Reader and click **Reports**.
2. Click **Reading Practice**.
3. Click on the name of the report.
4. Select options and click **View Report**.
5. Click **Print**.

Set the Preference for Printing the TOPS Report
Those with administrator access:
1. On the Renaissance Place Home page, scroll to Accelerated Reader and click **Preferences**.
2. Under School Preferences, click **Student Quizzing**.
3. Click **Edit Student Quizzing**.
4. Next to **TOPS Report Printing**, select options.
5. Click **Save**.

Those with teacher access (an administrator access must first set a preference to allow you to edit these options for your class):
1. On the Renaissance Place Home page, scroll to Accelerated Reader and click **Preferences**.
2. Under Classroom Preferences, click **Student Quizzing**.
3. Click **Edit Student Quizzing**.
4. In the drop-down menu under TOPS Report Printing, select **Classroom Settings**.
5. Select options by clicking in the boxes next to the RP (Reading Practice) pencil icon.
6. Click **Save**.

Reprint a TOPS Report
1. On the Renaissance Place Home page, scroll to Accelerated Reader and click **Class Record Books**.
2. Click **Reading Practice Quizzes**.
3. Click a student's name.
4. Under Actions, click **TOPS**.
5. Select English or Spanish. Click **Next**.
6. Click **Print** on the Adobe Acrobat Reader toolbar.

Using NEO 2 Laptops to Take AR Quizzes

Login as a Student and Take a Quiz
Before students can begin taking quizzes, you must install AlphaSmart Manager, connect the Renaissance Receiver to your computer, name the Renaissance Receiver, and set the Renaissance Place address in the wireless server utility. See the software manual for those instructions.
1. Turn on the NEO 2 by pressing **On/Off**; press **Applets**.
2. Press the down arrow until the cursor is next to Accelerated Reader; press **Enter**.
3. If necessary, use the up and down arrow keys to highlight the network (Receiver name) to which you must connect. Press **Enter**. (If you are asked if you want to stay connected to the last network used, press **Y** for yes or **N** for no. If you choose no, choose another network and press enter.)
4. Type the user name and press **Enter**, **Tab**, or the down arrow. Type the password and press **Enter**.
5. If necessary, use the up or down arrow to highlight the correct class; press **Enter**.

6. Use the up or down arrow to highlight the type of quiz you wish to take; press **Enter**.
7. Type the quiz number and press **Enter**.
8. If the quiz is in English and Spanish, use the arrow keys to select English; press **Enter**. (Spanish quizzes are not yet supported by NEO 2.)
9. If you are asked how the book was read, use the arrow keys to select an answer; press **Enter**.
10. When the quiz title appears, press **Y** for yes; press **Enter**.
11. For each question, press the letter of the answer you think is correct. Use the up and down arrow keys to scroll. Use tab or the left and right arrow key to switch between the question and answer panes.
12. Press **Enter** to go to the next question.
13. At the end of the quiz, answer any additional questions that may appear (for example, how you liked the quiz, which language you want the TOPS Report to appear in) and press **Enter**.
14. If you do not want to immediately take another quiz, press **N** for no; press **Enter**.

Renaissance Home Connect (AR Enterprise only)

Printing the Informational Letter

1. If Renaissance Home Connect is available to you, you will see a Renaissance Home Connect tab on the Renaissance Place Home page. Scroll to it and click **Informational Letter**.
2. Select students or classes. Click **View Letter**.
3. Click the Adobe Reader print icon. The software will automatically add student login information before printing.

Instructions for Common Software Tasks
Desktop Version

Using STAR Assessments

Log Into the STAR Reading or STAR Early Literacy Management Application and Work With Student Information

For those with administrator access:
1. Open the management application.
2. Enter your password.
3. Click **OK**.
4. Click the **Go** drop-down menu and click **Students**. Click **Add**. Enter student information. Click **OK**.
5. Click the **Go** drop-down menu and click **Students**. Click a student's name and click **Edit**. Make changes and click **OK**.

Add Classes

For those with administrator access:
1. Click the **Go** drop-down menu and click **Classes**.
2. Click **Add**. Enter the class name and password.
3. Click **Assign Teacher**. Select a teacher or click **New** to add a teacher and click **OK**.
4. Click **OK** again to finish.

Edit Classes
1. Click the Go drop-down menu and click **Classes**.
2. Click a class and click **Edit**. Make changes and click **OK**.

Enroll Students
1. Click the **Go** drop-down menu and click **Classes**.
2. Click a class and click **Enroll**.
3. To select one student, click on the student's name and click **Add**. To select a group of students listed consecutively, click the first student's name, hold down the Shift key and click the last student's name; click **Add**. To select a number of individual students throughout the list, click each student's name while holding down the Control key. (To first sort by grade, click **Grade**.) To add all students on the list, click **Add All**.
4. Click **OK**.

Set a Monitor Password for STAR Reading

For those with administrator access:
1. Click the **Go** drop-down menu and click **Preferences**.
2. Scroll to and click **Testing Password**. Click **Edit**. Choose an option. Click **OK**.

Set a Monitor Password for STAR Early Literacy
For those with administrator access:
1. Click the **Go** drop-down menu and click **Preferences**.
2. Scroll to and click the **Security** preference. Click **Edit**. Click the monitor field and type in the new password. Click **OK**.

Locate Pretest Instructions for STAR Reading
1. Click the **Start** menu. Scroll to Programs and STAR Reading. (On Macintosh computers, open the HD and Application folder.)
2. Click **Pretest Instructions**.

Log Into STAR Reading as a Student and Take a Test
1. Open the student application.
2. Click a class name and click **OK**.
3. Click a student's name and click **OK**.
4. Abort the test with **Ctrl A** (Windows) or **Open Apple A** (Macintosh).

Log Into STAR Early Literacy as a Student and Take a Test
1. Open the student application.
2. Click a class name and click **Login**.
3. Click a student's name and click **Login**. Enter a student password if asked and click **OK**. Enter a monitor password if asked and click **OK**. (The default monitor password is admin.)
4. Abort the test with **Ctrl A** (Windows) or **Open Apple A** (Macintosh).

View and Customize Reports and Locate Student Passwords
1. Click the **Go** drop-down menu and click **Reports**.
2. Click the name of the report you want to customize and click **Custom**. Follow the instructions on each screen. Select the option to include student passwords. Click **Finish**.

Working With AR Reading Practice Quizzes

Identify Students' Passwords
1. Click the **Go** drop-down menu. Under Classroom, click **Reports**.
2. Select your class.
3. Scroll to the Student List Report.
4. Click **Group** to choose classes and students.
5. Click **Options** and select the option to include passwords.
6. Click **Print**.

Log Into Accelerated Reader as a Student and Take a Reading Practice Quiz
1. Open the student application.
2. Click a class name and click **Login**.
3. Click a student's name and click **Login**.
4. Enter the student's password and click **OK**.
5. Click the type of quiz you would like to take.
6. Click the name of a quiz and click **Take Quiz**.
7. Confirm that you would like to take this quiz by clicking **Yes**.
8. Abort the quiz with **Ctrl A** (Windows) or **Open Apple A** (Macintosh).

Log Into the Management Application and Preview a Quiz
1. Log into the Management Application.
2. Click on **School** or click the **Go** drop-down menu.
3. Click **Quizzes**.
4. Click the name of a quiz.
5. Click **Preview**.
6. Click **Take A Sample Student Quiz**.

View Reading Practice Quiz Information
1. Click the **Go** drop-down menu. Under Classroom, click **Reading Practice**.
2. Click a class name.
3. Click a student's name. View the student's quiz information at the bottom of the screen.

Edit TWI Settings
For those with administrator access:
1. Click the **Go** drop-down menu. Under School, click **Preferences**.
2. Click **TWI Monitoring**.
3. Click **Edit**. Select **Enable TWI Monitoring** to turn on this preference.
4. Click **OK**.

For those with teacher access (an administrator must enable TWI monitoring for the school before you can adjust the setting for your class):
1. Click the **Go** drop-down menu. Under Classroom, click **Reading Practice**.
2. Click a student's name.
3. Click the **General** tab at the bottom of the screen.
4. Click **Edit TWI**. Choose an option.
5. Click **OK**.

Viewing Quiz Data and Printing Reports

Locate, View, and Print Reports
1. Click the **Go** drop-down menu. Under Classroom, click **Reports**.
2. Select your class.
3. Scroll to the report you wish to view or, to use the quick-find feature, start typing the name of the report.
4. Click **Group**, **Date**, and/or **Options**.
5. Select options and click **Print**.

Set the Preference for Printing the TOPS Report
For those with administrator access:
1. Click the **Go** drop-down menu. Under School, click **Preferences**.
2. Click **TOPS Report**.
3. Click **Edit** and select an option.
4. Click **OK**.

For those with teacher access (an administrator must first set a preference to allow you to edit this option for your class):
1. Click the **Go** drop-down menu. In the Classroom section, click **Preferences**.
2. Click **TOPS Report**.
3. Click **Edit** and select an option.
4. Click **OK**.

Reprint a TOPS Report
1. Click the **Go** drop-down menu. Under Classroom, click **Reading Practice**.
2. Select your class and click **OK**.
3. Click a student's name on the list at the top of the screen.
4. Click the **Quizzes** tab at the bottom of the screen. Choose a quiz and click on the title.
5. Click **Print TOPS**.

Setting Goals

Enter Student Goals
1. Enter marking periods using the School Year preference wizard.
2. Click the **Go** drop-down menu. Under Classroom, click **Reading Practice**.
3. Click a student's name on the list at the top of the screen.
4. Click the **Goals** tab at the bottom of the screen.
5. Click the marking period for which you want to set goals, and click **Set**.
6. Enter goals. Use the tab key to move from field to field.
7. Click **OK**.

Goal-Setting Chart

Use the chart and guidelines below to help plan goals for your students based on their reading level and the amount of daily reading practice that you provide.

Identify ZPD

Identify each student's grade-equivalent (GE) score with a standardized assessment, such as STAR Reading, or estimate a GE based on the student's past performance. The corresponding ZPD is a recommended book-level range for the student. If books in that range seem too hard or easy for a student, choose a new range or create a wider one that better matches the student's abilities.

Set Goals

Average percent correct—The most important goal for all students is to average 85% or higher on Reading Practice Quizzes. Meeting this goal has significant impact on reading growth. Averages of 90% and higher are associated with even greater gains. If a student struggles to maintain the minimum average, talk to the student and find out why. Then decide on a strategy that will lead to success.

Point goals—The chart shows the number of points students are expected to earn based on GE and time spent reading. These are estimates—set goals that are realistic for individual students.

Grade-Equivalent Score	Suggested ZPD	60 Min. Daily Practice			30 Min. Daily Practice			20 Min. Daily Practice		
		Points per Week	Points per 6 Weeks	Points per 9 Weeks	Points per Week	Points per 6 Weeks	Points per 9 Weeks	Points per Week	Points per 6 Weeks	Points per 9 Weeks
1.0	1.0 – 2.0	1.7	10	15	0.9	5.0	7.5	0.6	3.3	5.0
1.5	1.5 – 2.5	1.9	11	17	1.0	5.5	8.5	0.6	3.7	5.7
2.0	2.0 – 3.0	2.1	13	19	1.1	6.5	9.5	0.7	4.3	6.3
2.5	2.3 – 3.3	2.3	14	21	1.2	7.0	10.5	0.8	4.7	7.0
3.0	2.6 – 3.6	2.5	15	23	1.3	7.5	11.5	0.8	5.0	7.7
3.5	2.8 – 4.0	2.7	16	24	1.4	8.0	12.0	0.9	5.3	8.0
4.0	3.0 – 4.5	2.8	17	25	1.4	8.5	12.5	0.9	5.7	8.3
4.5	3.2 – 5.0	3.2	19	29	1.6	9.5	14.5	1.0	6.3	9.7
5.0	3.4 – 5.4	3.5	21	32	1.8	10.5	16.0	1.2	7.0	10.7
5.5	3.7 – 5.7	3.9	23	35	2.0	11.5	17.5	1.3	7.7	11.7
6.0	4.0 – 6.1	4.2	25	39	2.1	12.5	19.5	1.4	8.3	13.0
6.5	4.2 – 6.5	4.6	28	41	2.3	14.0	20.5	1.5	9.3	13.7
7.0	4.3 – 7.0	4.9	29	44	2.5	14.5	22.0	1.6	9.7	14.7
7.5	4.4 – 7.5	5.3	32	48	2.7	16.0	24.0	1.8	10.7	16.0
8.0	4.5 – 8.0	5.6	34	50	2.8	17.0	25.0	1.9	11.3	16.7
9.0	4.6 – 9.0	6.3	38	57	3.2	19.0	28.5	2.1	12.7	19.0
10.0	4.7 – 10.0	6.9	41	62	3.5	20.5	31.0	2.3	13.7	20.7
11.0	4.8 – 11.0	7.6	46	68	3.8	23.0	34.0	2.5	15.3	22.7
12.0	4.9 – 12.0	8.3	50	75	4.2	25.0	37.5	2.8	16.7	25.0

Reproducible Form © 2008 Renaissance Learning, Inc.

Goal-Setting Chart for ATOS 2000

Use the chart and guidelines below to help plan goals for your students based on their reading level and the amount of daily reading practice that you provide.

Identify ZPD

Identify each student's reading level with a standardized assessment, such as STAR Reading, or estimate a reading level based on the student's past performance. The corresponding ZPD is a recommended book-level range for the student. If books in that range seem too hard or easy for a student, choose a new range or create a wider one that better matches the student's abilities.

Set Goals

Average percent correct—The most important goal for all students is to average 85% or higher on Reading Practice Quizzes. Meeting this goal has significant impact on reading growth. Averages of 90% and higher are associated with even greater gains. If a student struggles to maintain the minimum average, talk to the student and find out why. Then decide on a strategy that will lead to success.

Point goals—The chart shows the number of points students are expected to earn based on reading level and time spent reading. These are estimates—set goals that are realistic for individual students.

Alternate Reading Level	Suggested ZPD	60 Min. Daily Practice			30 Min. Daily Practice			20 Min. Daily Practice		
		Points per Week	Points per 6 Weeks	Points per 9 Weeks	Points per Week	Points per 6 Weeks	Points per 9 Weeks	Points per Week	Points per 6 Weeks	Points per 9 Weeks
51	51 – 260	1.7	10	15	0.9	5.0	7.5	0.6	3.3	5.0
157	157 – 360	1.9	11	17	1.0	5.5	8.5	0.6	3.7	5.7
241	241 – 458	2.1	13	19	1.1	6.5	9.5	0.7	4.3	6.3
348	301 – 510	2.3	14	21	1.2	7.0	10.5	0.8	4.7	7.0
440	361 – 560	2.5	15	23	1.3	7.5	11.5	0.8	5.0	7.7
530	401 – 630	2.7	16	24	1.4	8.0	12.0	0.9	5.3	8.0
619	440 – 719	2.8	17	25	1.4	8.5	12.5	0.9	5.7	8.3
701	479 – 799	3.2	19	29	1.6	9.5	14.5	1.0	6.3	9.7
781	511 – 859	3.5	21	32	1.8	10.5	16.0	1.2	7.0	10.7
860	561 – 898	3.9	23	35	2.0	11.5	17.5	1.3	7.7	11.7
921	619 – 940	4.2	25	39	2.1	12.5	19.5	1.4	8.3	13.0
979	650 – 988	4.6	28	41	2.3	14.0	20.5	1.5	9.3	13.7
1029	669 – 1039	4.9	29	44	2.5	14.5	22.0	1.6	9.7	14.7
1080	681 – 1087	5.3	32	48	2.7	16.0	24.0	1.8	10.7	16.0
1121	701 – 1129	5.6	34	50	2.8	17.0	25.0	1.9	11.3	16.7
1201	720 – 1210	6.3	38	57	3.2	19.0	28.5	2.1	12.7	19.0
1293	731 – 1299	6.9	41	62	3.5	20.5	31.0	2.3	13.7	20.7
1364	750 – 1370	7.6	46	68	3.8	23.0	34.0	2.5	15.3	22.7
1434	769 – 1440	8.3	50	75	4.2	25.0	37.5	2.8	16.7	25.0

Reproducible Form © 2008 Renaissance Learning, Inc.

Student Reading Log—With Goals

Student Name: _____ Points: _____ ZPD: _____ Class: _____

Goals: Average Percent Correct _____ Average Book Level _____

Quiz No.	Title	Book Level	Points	F/NF	Date	Pages Read		Teacher Review/ % Correct	Teacher Notes
						Begin-End	Total		

Registro de Lecturas—con las Metas

Nombre del Estudiante: _____ Clase: _____

Metas: Porcentaje de Promedio Correcto _____ Puntos: _____ ZPD: _____

Promedio del Nivel del Libro _____

Examen No.	Título	Nivel del libro	Puntos	F/NF	Fecha	Páginas leídas Inicio-Final	Páginas leídas Total	Revisión del Maestro[a]/ % Correcto	Comentarios del Maestro[a]

Student Reading Log—Emergent Reader

Student Name: _____

ZPD: Read To _____ Read With _____ Read Ind. _____

Date	Quiz No.	Title	Author	Book Level	Initial One			Monitor's Initials	% Correct	Teacher Notes
					Read To	Read With	Read Ind.			

Reproducible Form © 2008 Renaissance Learning, Inc.

Registro de Lecturas—Lector Emergente

Nombre del Estudiante: _____   ZPD: Leer A (T) _____   Leer Con (W) _____   Leer Ind. (I) _____

Fecha	Examen No.	Título	Autor	Nivel del libro	Seleccione Uno			Iniciales del Ayudante	% Correcto	Comentarios del Maestro[a]
					A / T	Con / W	Ind / I			

Reproducible Form © 2008 Renaissance Learning, Inc.

Student Reading Log—Beginning Reader

Student Name: _____ ZPD: Read To _____ Read With _____ Read Ind. _____

Date	Quiz Number	Title	Book Level	TWI	Monitor's Initials	% Correct	Teacher's Comments

Registro de Lecturas—Lector Principiante

Nombre del Estudiante: _____

ZPD: Leer A (T) _____ Leer Con (W) _____ Leer Ind. (I) _____

Fecha	Examen No.	Título	Nivel del libro	TWI	Iniciales del Ayudante	% Correcto	Comentarios del Maestro[a]

Reproducible Form © 2008 Renaissance Learning, Inc.

R.C.W.

Name: _____

Grade/Section: _____

Read a few pages.

Close your book.

Write what you remember.

R.C.W.

Name: _____

Grade/Section: _____

Read a few pages.

Close your book.

Write what you remember.

R.C.W.

Name: _____

Grade/Section: _____

Read a few pages.

Close your book.

Write what you remember.

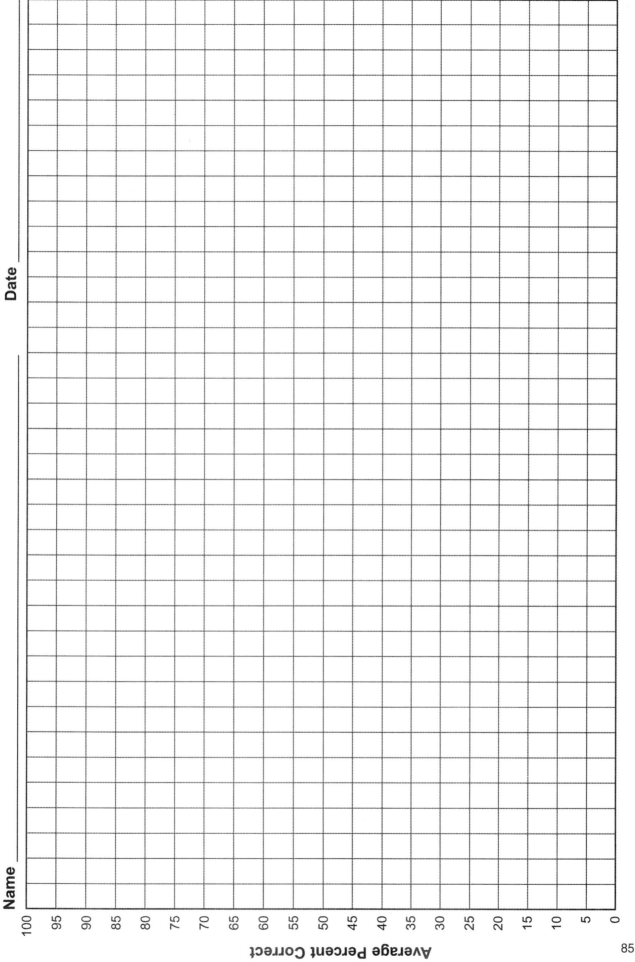

POINT GOAL CHART

Name _____ Date _____

Points

Week

Points

Accelerated Reader™

Reproducible Form © 2008 Renaissance Learning, Inc.

Status of the Class Record Sheet

Teacher _____ Class _____ Dates _____

STUDENT NAME	MONDAY	TUESDAY	WEDNESDAY	THURSDAY	FRIDAY	MONDAY	TUESDAY	WEDNESDAY	THURSDAY	FRIDAY

A = Absent   I = Intervention Needed   _ = OK

Reproducible Form © 2008 Renaissance Learning, Inc.

Classroom Practices in the Primary Grades

Keep a Classroom Library
Maintain a classroom library so that students can select books quickly and easily. Ask your school librarian to help you choose a collection of books that you can check out to your classroom. Select new books regularly, and keep popular titles longer so your students can read and reread their favorites. Also take advantage of book clubs and used bookstores to build your collection.

Color Code Books
Label Accelerated Reader books with colored dots to help young students find books within their ZPD. For example, you might label books at a 1.0–1.5 level with a yellow dot, at a 1.6–2.0 level with a red dot, and so on.

Set Up Activity Centers
Use one center as a location for teaching reading skills. Set up volunteers at another center and dedicate it to read alouds. At a third center, station an older student or parent volunteer to help students take quizzes.

Build Reading Skills with Read To, Read With, and Independent Reading Practice
Be sure to involve students in all three types of reading practice. Emergent readers will spend most of their reading time listening to stories and looking at picture books. As their skills develop, pair students with peer or adult tutors for Read With practice. Later, as students start reading independently, schedule short periods of independent practice time, along with plenty of Read To and Read With practice.

Recruit Volunteers and Quiz Monitors
Volunteers are essential to reading practice in the primary grades. Parents, retirees, even older students can read to and with students and help them take quizzes. Provide training sessions for volunteers to familiarize them with Accelerated Reader, ZPDs, student reading logs, and other classroom routines.

Teach Students How to Take Quizzes
Read an AR book aloud to your entire class. Then take all your students to one computer and introduce them to the Reading Practice Quiz. Explain that for each question they will choose an answer from a list of possible answers, and that they shouldn't pick an answer until they hear all the choices. After you read each question and the answer choices, have students come up with the correct answer together; you click the answer, explaining what you are doing. Do whole-group quizzing for a number of books. After that, you might divide the class into smaller groups and have students take turns clicking on the answer. After a period of practice, students will then be able to take quizzes individually, though they may need help as explained below.

Have Students Quiz the Same Way They Read
Make sure students take Reading Practice Quizzes the same way they read books. If you read a book *to* a student, also read the quiz *to* him. If you read *with* a student, make sure the student reads the quiz *with* you or a volunteer. Students can also use Recorded Voice Quizzes to quiz on books that were read to or with them.

Monitor Reading Practice
Keep an eye on your students' reading practice by reviewing reading logs and TOPS Reports every day. (See pages 78-83 for examples of logs for emergent, beginning, and established readers.) Set up a simple book checkout system for your classroom library so that you can also see if the books individual students are selecting are a good match.

Set Goals for All Readers
While students are in the emergent-reader stage, you may set a general point goal of at least .5 points (for kindergartners) or .75 points a week (for first graders). Once students are reading independently, set personalized goals based on reading ability.

Index

average percent correct
  acknowledging, 40, 51
  and 100 percent scores, 36, 40, 51
  and reading gains, 35
  below 85 percent, 32
  chart, 39, 85
  85 percent and ZPD, 9, 18-19
  monitoring, 50
  goal, 57
  value of 90 percent and higher, 9, 29-30, 35-36

baseline data, 7, 16
BookFinder, 43
book level
  adjusting, 18
  alternate scales for, 8, 57
  definition of, 8
  goal, 57-58
  in point formula, 8
  monitoring, 28, 31, 32, 33
  on labels, 14
  on Student Reading Log, 26
  ZPD and, 17-18
book selection, 6, 15, 18, 23, 32, 33, 47
book talks, 42
bulletin boards, 40

choice, importance of, 18, 30, 37
color-code, 14
comprehension
  assessment with AR quizzes, 6, 13, 18, 28, 62
  importance of, 9, 35
  in a balanced reading program, 5
  listening, 24
  monitoring, 28, 32, 36
  strategies, 5, 9, 19, 24, 30, 32, 36-37, 57
Comprehension Goal Chart, 39, 85
computers, 15, 48

diagnostic code, 31, 50, 61
Diagnostic Report, 31, 39, 50, 60

emergent readers, 19-20, 21
engaged time, 34

English-language learners, 21, 24, 32, 33
feedback, 6, 29, 38, 62
folder, 47, 48, 58

goals
  additional, 57-59
  adjusting, 22, 23
  book-level, 57-58
  entering in software, 21
  for high-ability readers, 21
  making visible, 38-40
  monitoring, 31
  percent-correct, 9, 57, 85
  point, 8-9, 20-21, 26, 28, 32, 33, 39, 86
  recognition for achieving, 51
Goal-Setting Chart, 20, 21, 32, 57, 76-77
grades, 22

high-ability readers, 21
high school, 23
Home Connect, 41

independent reading, 6, 23, 27, 31, 36, 61
instruction, 5, 6, 23, 36, 62
interest level, 8, 14, 28, 33, 53

labeling books, 14
Lexiles (see book level, alternate scales for)
library
  access, 15
  collection, 33, 60, 88
  number of books needed, 14
Literacy Skills Quizzes, 62
log (See Student Reading Log)

Marzano, Robert, 6
model classroom certification, 59
monitoring
  with AR reports, 29-31, 50, 60-61
  with Status of the Class, 27-28, 36
  with Student Reading Log, 26-27
motivation, 29, 33, 38

National Reading Panel, 6
NEO 2, 15, 49

Other Reading Quizzes, 13, 62

passwords, 13
Point Goal Chart, 39, 86
points
    as a measure of practice, 8-9
    formula for calculating, 8
    goals for, 20-21, 57
    low number earned, 33
    on reports, 30, 31, 61
    on Student Reading Log, 26
    problems with, 9
practice
    importance of, 5
    managing, 26-33
    measuring, 9
    monitoring, 26-33
    personalizing, 5, 7-9, 16-21
    time for, 23-24
    types of, 23-24
pretest instructions, 16
primary grades, 14, 21, 24, 88-89

quiz-taking strategies, 24, 36-37
quizzing, 13, 23-24, 28, 32, 48-49, 52-53, 88-89

RCW booklets, 36, 84
Reading Practice Quizzes, 6, 13, 19, 31, 62
Reading Range Report, 16
reading to students, 19, 23-24, 42
reading with students, 19, 23-24
Renaissance Place, 13, 50, 67

self-directed learning, 30
self-monitoring, 24, 36
software instructions
    desktop version, 72
    Renaissance Place version, 67
STAR Early Literacy, 16
STAR Reading
    and goal setting, 57-58
    baseline data from, 7, 16, 52
    number of times to administer, 57
    ZPDs from, 16-17, 19, 32, 36, 57
Status of the Class
    and comprehension strategies, 36
    importance of, 50
    procedure, 27-28
    reinforcing instruction with, 36

Status of the Class Record Sheet, 50, 87
Student Information Report, 13
Student List Report, 13
Student Reading Log
    and goals, 26-27, 78-79
    as library pass, 15, 27
    during Status of the Class, 27-28
    how to use, 26-28, 47-49
    in reading folder, 47-49
    reproducable forms, 78-83
    to make success visible, 38
    when quizzing, 26, 48-49
Student Record Report, 38, 58, 60-61
summarizing, 32, 36, 42
sustained silent reading, 27

textbook reading, 18, 62
time for reading
    and goals, 20
    maximizing, 47-48
    recommendations, 23
    relationship to points, 9, 20
    scheduling, 6, 23, 54
TOPS Report, 29-30, 38, 47, 49
TWI Report, 61

user name, 13

vocabulary, 6, 8, 16, 17, 32, 42, 62
Vocabulary Practice Quizzes, 62

Wall of Fame, 40

zone of proximal development (ZPD)
    adjusting, 19, 32, 33, 37, 58
    and AR quiz averages, 18-19
    and book level, 57-58
    and emergent readers, 19-20
    and points, 20-21
    and self-direction, 18
    as a range, 17
    definition, 7
    how configured, 17-18
    identifying, 7, 16-18, 58
    monitoring, 28-33
    on Student Reading Log, 26
    reading outside, 32, 37, 53